Discovering Shakespeare

A Midsummer Night's Dream

A WORKBOOK FOR STUDENTS

YOUNG ACTORS SERIES

If you require pre-publication information about upcoming Smith and Kraus books, you may receive our semi-annual catalogue, free of charge, by sending your name and address to Smith and Kraus Catalogue, 4 Lower Mill Road, North Stratford, NH 03590. Or call us at (800) 895-4331, fax (603) 922-3348, e-mail SandK@sover.net, or check our website at WWW.SmithandKraus.Com

Discovering Shakespeare

A Midsummer Night's Dream

A WORKBOOK FOR STUDENTS

Written and Edited by
Fredi Olster and Rick Hamilton

Young Actors Series

SK

A Smith and Kraus Book

A Smith and Kraus Book
Published by Smith and Kraus, Inc.
One Main Street, PO Box 127, Lyme, NH 03768

Copyright © 1996 by F. Olster and R. Hamilton
All rights reserved
Manufactured in the United States of America
Cover and Text Design by Julia Hill
Cover Art by Irene Kelly

First Edition: June 1996
10 9 8 7 6 5 4 3 2

Library of Congress Cataloging-in-Publication Date

Discovering Shakespeare: A midsummer night's dream : a workbook for students / edited by Fredi Olster and Rick Hamilton. --1st ed. p. cm. --
(Young actors series, ISSN 1067-3261)
Includes an abridgement of the original text, an adaptation into vernacular English, and discussions of Shakespearean English, character analysis, and performance and production.
Includes bibliographical references (p.).
Summary: A guide to reading, understanding, and performing Shakespeare's A midsummer night's dream.
ISBN 1-57525-042-X (pbk.)
1. Shakespeare, William, 1564-1616, Midsummer night's dream.
2. Shakespeare, William,1564-1616--Problems, exercises, etc.
3. Shakespeare, William,1564-1616--Outlines, syllabi, etc.
4. Shakespeare, William,1564-1616--Dramatic production.
5. Shakespeare, William,1564-1616--Adaptations.
[1. Shakespeare, William, 1564-1616. Midsummer night's dream. 2. Shakespeare, William, 1564-1616--Dramatic production.]
I. Olster, Fredi. II. Hamilton, Rick. III. Series: Young actor series.
PR2827.D55   1996
822.3'3--dc20   96-15955
CIP
AC

Contents

"How came these things to pass?"

HOW THESE BOOKS CAME
TO BE WRITTEN

I have spent most of my life working as a Shakespearean actress. Yet, when I was growing up and studying Shakespeare in school, I hated it! I came to realize that many of my teachers also hated it. And who can blame any of us, we didn't understand it for the most part.

It wasn't until I started acting in Shakespeare's plays at the Oregon Shakespeare Festival in 1970 that I began to feel differently. There, I met Angus Bowmer, the founder of the festival and director of the first play I was to do there, *The Merchant of Venice,* and Rick Hamilton, a young actor at the festival, who was later to become my husband.

Between them, they taught me to love the language and to appreciate the timelessness of the stories. And now, of course, I'm hooked. I would rather act in a play by Shakespeare than any other playwright.

I've come to realize that my experience with Shakespeare is not unique. And it was my desire to share what I have learned from Angus and Rick and the many other directors and actors I've worked with over the years that inspired me to write this workbook.

The immediate impetus came though while I was doing a production of *Christmas Carol* in San Francisco. I was playing Mrs. Fezziwig who is a delightful character but who isn't in a lot of scenes. So I had a great deal of time for other activities.

One of them was to start work on *All's Well That Ends Well,* which I was to be in when *Christmas Carol* closed. "All's Well" was a play that I was totally unfamiliar with. I was sitting in my dressing room with my Shakespeare glossaries, dictionaries and various copies of the play doing my *homework* when my friend Sarah came in and asked what I was up to.

Sarah was then twelve and was playing Young Belle in our production. She and I were old friends having worked together on two shows in the past. I told Sarah what I was doing and she asked if she could read "All's Well" with me. I said "sure" and we proceeded to read the Helena/Parolles scene in Act 1 together.

Note that this is a particularly difficult scene, full of double-entendre, sexual innuendo and very complex language. We read together and looked up all the words we didn't grasp.

Let me say that I have to do this whenever I work on a Shakespeare play that I don't know well. The words he used are different from the ones we now use. In the four hundred years since he wrote these plays, the English language has changed and some of the words Shakespeare used have gone out of fashion or have evolved in their meanings so that we no longer easily understand them.

But with a little practice and *homework* we quickly realize that the ideas he wrote about remain extremely applicable to us.

I came to understand this even more clearly when, after Sarah and I had finished the scene and had discussed what it meant, Sarah said to me, "I'm going to read this to my friends tomorrow at school, this stuff is great and it's so sexy." Well at that moment I realized once again the absolute brilliance of Shakespeare. He had the power to reach out through those four hundred years that separated him and Sarah and thoroughly excite her interest.

Sarah is now a young lady of fourteen and not only has she continued to be excited by Shakespeare, but she has passed on her interest to her younger sister Julia who is ten.

The question then became, how can we (by this time Rick agreed to work on this project with me) make Shakespeare accessible to kids who don't have an actor to sit down and read it with? And that's how the idea for this format came about.

Our objective became: tell the story, introduce the characters, and let Shakespeare's ideas come ringing through. The difficulty, of course, is that wonderfully complex language of Shakespeare's. So we decided, the best way to introduce Shakespeare to people who were not familiar with him was, as I had done with Sarah, to translate him into the *vernacular*—that is, our equivalent everyday language.

That way, the new student of Shakespeare can begin to understand the story, the characters and the ideas without the added obstacle of the four-hundred-year-old words.

Once these elements become clearer and the reader starts to discover the beauty of Shakespeare, as Sarah did, it then becomes even more thrilling to go back to the original language which is, needless to say, so much richer and more poetic than anything we have replaced it with.

Let us point out here that this workbook is only meant as an introduction to Shakespeare. We are actors and not scholars and would not pretend competency in that world.

Our main objective is to instill a love of Shakespeare and to encourage the next generation of young people to attend our theatres with a true desire to see and support and perhaps act in the works of the incomparable master.

It is our sincere hope that the users of these workbooks will discover the joys of Shakespeare sooner than we were able to and will be tempted to move on to Shakespeare's complete versions of the plays with enthusiasm and with ease.

How To Use This Book

The Discovering Shakespeare edition of *A Midsummer Night's Dream,* with its abridged version of the play along with the vernacular translation and supportive chapters, is designed for multiple uses.

1). It serves as a workbook to help in the study of Shakespeare's language. By reading scenes aloud, and using the accompanying vernacular translation to facilitate comprehension, the student will find it easier to understand the language and plot of the play thereby making the study of Shakespeare an enjoyable experience.

2). It serves as a launching pad for a *reading* of the play. Students take on the individual parts, doing research into the characters and then, with scripts in hand, read the play aloud.

3). It serves as an aid in organizing a simple production of the play for classroom performance.

It is up to the facilities available and the interest of the various class situations to determine what would be most useful for them.

We have included information about *performance* because this material is vital for the understanding of Shakespeare. Shakespeare was first and foremost a man of the theatre. To understand him, it is necessary to understand the medium he was writing for.

It is our intention that the vernacular version be employed to facilitate understanding of Shakespeare's language, and that Shakespeare's own words be used for performance.

Also, please note that the suggested stage directions, acting notes, character interpretations etc. reflect our personal opinions and should merely be thought of as a starting place—none of this is in stone—Shakespeare is open to interpretation. Be free and creative in your choices and your work. You are the next generation of Shakespeare students, interpreters, audience and performers—he is now in your hands—serve him well.

"*" within the play indicates suggestion to see chapter on acting techniques and theatrical conventions

"First say what the play treats on…"
A LOOK AT SOME OF THE IDEAS IN *"DREAM"*

In *A Midsummer Night's Dream,* Shakespeare transports us to Athens almost three thousand years ago. Why Athens? During Shakespeare's time the glories of ancient Greece and Rome were being rediscovered. Mathematics, philosophy, art, theatre and the classical ideas of how to live life, long buried, were reemerging and people all over Europe were fascinated.

Athens was a focal point for these ideas, one of which stated that man's ability to reason set him apart from other countries and that reason dictated a life of balance and moderation.

It is against this background of rationality and reasonableness that Shakespeare chooses to set a play about love, one of the most irrational, unreasonable occurrences on the face of the earth!

With a gleam in his eye, with laughter that helps us to see ourselves more clearly, and with just a little bit of magic, Shakespeare sets out to show us how otherwise reasonable, balanced humans (and fairies) behave when in love.

It is our passions and desires which drive us to seek relationships, but reason must temper these in order to prevent excesses. It is this ever fluid balance between reason and passion that Shakespeare explores in *Dream*.

He offers examples of love out of balance as embodied in the various pairs of lovers in the play, and shows these relationships progressing towards balance over the course of time.

Theseus and Hippolyta have literally been at war, an unreasonable situation to be sure. Theseus has won the war, captured Hippolyta and brought her back to Athens. Whether he plans to marry her because he loves her, or in order to affect a peace is not made clear. Nor are Hippolyta's feelings—is she an entirely willing partner? Has she been swept off her feet by the indomitable warrior Theseus? Or is she merely going along with the marriage for the sake of decorum and peace? The language they use indicates a rather formal marriage, one that will serve political necessity rather than passion. This is an example of a relationship where passion has become subordinated to reason, workable, but not necessarily satisfying to the heart.

All the action of *Dream* takes place between the announcement of Theseus and Hippolyta's marriage and the celebration of it. It is what brings Titania and Oberon to town; what causes the workmen to prepare their play; and it is the deadline of the wedding day that precipitates Lysander and Hermia's elopement.

With the young lovers, Shakespeare gives us other perspectives of balance. Demetrius is a young man who has not learned to be satisfied with what he has. He's the kind of guy who if he had a BMW, he'd want a Ferrari, if he had a Ferrari he'd want a Mercedes. Unfortunately, he is the same with women. He craves whomever he doesn't have. He is in danger of becoming a Don Juan. He is definitely out of balance and needs to stop and take stock of himself.

Demetrius' last conquest was Helena and while he thinks he has moved on to Hermia, Helena has other plans. She is tenacious and believes she has found her true-love and is not about to let him go. She is totally unreasonable in her pursuit of Demetrius. Were she rational at this point she might realize that anyone who treated her the way

Demetruis had, should not be given a second chance—but not our Helena. Oh, no! She puts her pain on parade, so much so that even Theseus has heard of it. She is a prime example of how love can make one behave in an unreasonable, out of balance way.

Helena is a comic character to be sure, but it is important to know why we laugh at her. She has been *dumped* and that hurts. Shakespeare is not making fun of her pain, but of her reaction to her pain.

Hermia, on the other hand, is a girl of a different sort. Hermia is as solid as Helena is soft and sentimental. She wants Lysander and Lysander wants her and that's all there is to it. And there's the rub. Her father, who has complete legal control over her, says *no*.

Lysander, while not as headstrong as Hermia, is committed to his love for her and together, they hatch a plan to elope that flies in the face of all conventions of the time for the sake of their love.

They are perhaps the most *balanced* of our couples; he loves her, she loves him. Under normal circumstances both are well behaved respectful young people—but throw *love* in that mixture and suddenly you have a willingness to sacrifice all!

It is the outside pressure upon their love that has destroyed their otherwise normal existences and pushed them to these extreme means.

As the play moves from day to night, we meet the next and perhaps most important pair of lovers. Titania and Oberon are two of the most alluring creatures ever created. They are immortal, have numerous powers and yet they are all too *human*.

Their quarrel stems from infidelity or at least suspected infidelity. Shakespeare never says that they have actually committed adultery, but they have definitely had their heads turned. Small wonder, if you've been married for 100,000 years, you might get a little bored too—but no matter who started it, the results are disastrous!

Titania's speech beautifully demonstrates how the whole world begins to wobble then crash and burn when men and women are not in harmony.

> The spring, the summer,
> The childing autumn, angry winter, change
> Their wonted liveries, and the mazed world
> By their increase now knows not which is which.
> And this same progency of evils comes
> From our debate, from our dissension;
> We are their parents and original.

The play concerns how harmony and balance are

achieved in these relationships and how difficult this process can be. So difficult as to require MAGIC! This magic perhaps being the ability of the heart to forgive.

The play's happy and festive ending is the result of this restoration. The dark night of the soul has passed; a new morning will come.

There is one more aspect of the play we want to consider here. It is an idea that Shakespeare returns to time and again throughout his writings. It is best expressed by Shakespeare himself in *Hamlet* when the title character tells a friend:

There are more things in heaven and earth, Horatio,
Than are dreamt of in your philosophy.
(Act 1 scene 5)

In *A Midsummer Night's Dream* Shakespeare has created worlds within worlds of ever expanding awareness. Consider this. In the fifth act, we have Pyramus and Thisbe and their story being performed by Bottom and company, being watched by the court of lovers, who are in turn being watched by the fairies, who are in turn being watched by us, the audience, who are in turn being watched by..........?

"What are they that do play it"
BRIEF DESCRIPTIONS OF THE CHARACTERS IN "DREAM"

A Midsummer Night's Dream is a magical fantasy involving three distinct groups of characters. The first group we meet includes people from the upper class of Athens. They include Theseus, Hippolyta, Egeus, Hermia, Lysander, Demetrius, Helena and Philostrate.

The second group is made up of workingmen of Athens: Bottom, a weaver, Quince, a carpenter, Flute, a bellows-mender, Snout, a tinker, Snug, a joiner, and Starveling, a tailor.

The third is composed of members of the fairy world. These include Titania, Oberon, Puck and their fairies.

Let's look at each character individually.

THESEUS:

Theseus is the Duke of Athens. Athens was the most important city in the ancient Greek world and therefore we might think of Theseus as the equivalent of the president of the United States.

At the opening of the play, we discover that he has recently returned from a war during which he captured Hippolyta, the Queen of the Amazons, and now, as a way of cementing the peace between their nations, he and Hippolyta are to be married.

Theseus is a mature, thoughtful and compassionate ruler. He carries out the laws of his land with fairness. We see him demonstrate these traits throughout the course of the play. In Act One scene 1, rather then just arbitrarily imposing the sentence of celibacy or death on her, he gives Hermia time to think through her feelings by postponing the sentence until the day of his marriage.

He also makes a point of taking Egeus and Demetrius with him when he leaves, thus giving Lysander and Hermia some time alone to discuss their situation.

We later see his compassion demonstrated when he overturns the law and allows Hermia and Lysander to be married.

Still, another example of his fairness and kindness towards his subjects is illustrated when in Act 5 Philostrate makes fun of the workmen who want to perform their play and Theseus insists, "I will hear that play."

Note also that Theseus is guided in all that he does by his rationality and his reason. He is not a man who is inclined to flights of fantasy or whimsy. His view of the world is the real, the concrete vision.

HIPPOLYTA:

Hippolyta is Queen of the Amazons, a race of female warriors. She and her army have been conquered by Theseus and his troops in battle. Theirs is a "political" marriage. It will seal a peace for their lands.

Hippolyta is perhaps the first female version of "the strong silent type." She looks forward to her marriage with none of the youthful intensity Hermia and Helena display, nor does she show any of the jealous passion we see with Titania. Her relationship with Theseus appears to be the mature, intellectual, unfrenzied version of love.

EGEUS:

Egeus is a prosperous citizen of Athens. He might, in modern day terms, be an influential senator or lawyer in Washington D.C. (note his obsession with the law.) In any case he has easy access to the Duke and they obviously know each other well.

His anger towards Lysander may seem at first to be without rational basis. But, if we examine his first speech to the Duke, we realize that what probably happened is that Demetrius came to him and asked for permission to woo Hermia. Egeus granted him permission not knowing that Lysander and Hermia had already been seeing each other.

When Hermia told her father of her developing relationship with Lysander, he was furious because Lysander had not first come to him to ask his permission.

At this point, Egeus, perhaps upset by the realization that his little girl is growing up and that he is about to lose her, becomes totally irrational and stubborn. And this is the state he is in when we first meet him.

THE LOVERS:

With the four young lovers, we have a situation which is very common. There are two young girls who have been best friends from the time they were toddlers and now as they approach young womanhood they become interested in boys and everything changes.

HERMIA:

Hermia is the more socially adept of the two young women. She is vivacious, charming, friendly, outgoing and happy. Because of these traits she is the one that all the young boys want to date. She probably is also a bit of a natural flirt.

She is definitely Egeus' daughter. She has her own very strong stubborn streak which she no doubt picked up from him. She has strong feelings and she shows her willingness to stand up for them—both when she says she will live a virgin rather than marry someone she doesn't love and then when she decides to run off with Lysander. These are extremely daring things for a young girl in her society to do.

We also see evidence of her loyal trusting nature exhibited throughout the play. For example, when she wakes and finds Lysander gone, she never doubts him for a moment and is convinced that Demetrius must have murdered him. She is so steadfast in her belief in Lysander, that he has to practically "spell it out" to convince her that he is in love with Helena in Act 3.

It is at this point that we discover another aspect of Hermia's character—her spitfire temper. When she turns on Demetrius and then on Helena in Act 3 scene 2, she displays such ferocity that it almost takes us by surprise. This is reinforced by Helena when she says that "she was a vixen when she went to school."

LYSANDER:

Lysander also comes from the upper class of Athens. He tells us that his family is as well-off as Demetrius' and we soon learn that he has a wealthy aunt and he is her only heir.

Lysander seems to be an easy going young man, not prone to action till pushed. It takes a good deal of prodding from Hermia before he comes up with the idea to elope.

He also seems to be quite studious. He refers to his reading about "the course of true love." We also see that he is fairly mature and is definitely more serious about things than is Demetrius. He has found his true-love and is totally loyal to her, as opposed to Demetrius who seems pretty fickle.

Lysander is also very practical. Once he has come to the conclusion that he and Hermia must elope, he methodically plans their departure from Athens in order to be free of the law that threatens them.

There is another side to Lysander that is slightly bumbling or inept. We see this demonstrated when he loses his way in the woods on the way to his aunt's house (his planning was better than his execution) and then again when he doesn't quite know how to shake loose of Hermia when he wants to go off and fight with Demetrius. Perhaps these gentle qualities are the very things that Hermia loves him for.

DEMETRIUS:

Demetrius is the character who causes the entire story of the lovers to take place. If it were not for his actions regarding his transfer of affections from Helena to Hermia, there would be no conflict in this circle of lovers and therefore no reason for Egeus to come to Theseus and begin the course of events that start the play.

Demetrius can perhaps be described as a wealthy spoiled "brat" who wants his own way and refuses to take "no" for an answer.

What do we learn about Demetrius from the script? We know that Demetrius courted Helena and then switched his pursuit to Hermia. There are many questions we can ask about this situation:

1) Is there something about Helena that drove him off, or does her commitment to him frighten him?

2) Is there something about Hermia that is irresistible to Demetrius?

3) Does Demetrius just want what he cannot have?

4) Is Demetrius vying for power with Lysander and therefore wants what Lysander has?

There are no wrong or right answers to these questions, but, by exploring them, we can make some decisions about the character of Demetrius.

We do know that Egeus has given his consent for Demetrius to marry Hermia which tells us that, at least from an adult point of view, Demetrius is a desirable catch. Theseus, too, points out that he is a "worthy" gentleman. What does puzzle us though is why, in the face of clear rejection from Hermia, Demetrius chooses to continue, so publicly, in his pursuit of her.

Another thing we notice about Demetrius is his bluntness and his rudeness particularly in his dealing with Helena. It takes Oberon's *intervention* to *make a man* of Demetrius. And when he does finally *come to his senses*—both literally and figuratively after waking in the forest, he has been transformed into a wonderfully sensitive and mature young man.

With this in mind, we see that Demetrius perhaps best embodies Shakespeare's idea that "things base and vile holding no quantity, love can transpose to form and dignity." Once Demetrius' transformation is accomplished, harmony comes to the lover's story.

HELENA:

Helena is the daughter of Nedar, a man we hear referred to but never meet in the course of the play. Her social situation is pretty much the same as Hermia's. We know that Hermia and Helena have been best friends since earliest childhood, and at this time friendships would be formed within the same social strata.

When we meet Helena, we are probably seeing her at her very worst. She is *lovesick!* She is hopelessly in love with a guy who is in love with her best friend.

Helena is particularly obsessive in her love. She is persistent to the extreme. As Lysander says she "dotes, devoutly dotes, dotes in idolatry" upon Demetrius. This coming from the honest, straightforward Lysander says a lot!

Helena does have some moments of self-aware-ness in the midst of her misery. She realizes the absurdity of her situation. She talks about love's powers and realizes that love cannot be rationally explained.

But even with her flashes of insight, Helena is still pretty frustrating to deal with because she is forever attempting to manipulate situations to benefit herself. We see this in Act 2 scene 1 with Demetrius; he quite plainly tells her that he is not interested in her. Helena, quickly turns this around and proceeds to blame Demetrius for being so attractive, thereby forcing her to be drawn to him.

Poor Helena is so insecure at the time we encounter her that she doubts everything about herself. She is convinced that she is unattractive even though we learn from what the other characters say about her that she and Hermia are both pretty. It is this self doubt that consumes Helena and drives her actions through the play until equilibrium is restored with the aid of the fairy juice and the magical night in the forest.

We then finally see Helena's newfound maturity expressed with her line, "I have found Demetrius like a jewel, mine own and not mine own." With this brilliantly simple statement, Helena and Shakespeare are telling us a profound thing about the nature of love. Just as one cannot truly *possess* a jewel (since the jewel's beauty is intrinsic to the jewel and cannot be *owned* by anyone but only *appreciated* for a time) so one cannot *possess* the person one loves but only share in that other person's life.

By the end of the play when Demetrius and Helena have acknowledged their love for each other, Helena has come to realize that she cannot *own* Demetrius as she had hoped to at the start of the play and she is content with that.

PHILOSTRATE:

Philostrate's position in the Duke's household can probably best be described as the equivalent of the chief of staff at the White House. He is the person who arranges the Duke's schedule and acts as a sort of social secretary for the Duke. He seems to be a bit of a snob as we see in the condescending manner in which he refers to the efforts of the workmen of Athens.

THE WORKMEN:

We now come to the workmen of Athens. These are the fellows who literally labor with their hands. They are the craftsmen of the town. As Philostrate describes them they are "hard-handed men that work in Athens, which never labored in their minds till now"—not the brightest bunch of guys!

They probably began as apprentices to a master and now are masters themselves or, as with the young Flute, still apprenticing.

They are subjects of the Duke and are planning to prepare a play to help celebrate the Duke and Hippolyta's wedding day.

It was customary for the people of a city to pay tribute to their leader at such special times. But it is perhaps unusual that these non-actors should select a play as their offering. It also should be noted that such offerings were given with the hope that the Duke would be so moved by them that he would reward the participants with some sort of stipend.

These are simple, earthy people. They walk and talk differently than the courtly folk, perhaps even slouching or speaking with lower-class accents.

QUINCE:

Peter Quince is a carpenter. He is also the organizer of this undertaking. He is the one who has assembled the cast list, prepared the scripts, arranged for the rehearsal site and is acting as the *director.* We see him in this position doing all those things a director must do: encouraging, cajoling, and mollifying his actors, attempting to solve the problems presented in the script and actually conducting the rehearsal.

Quince seems to be a good-hearted, earnest, hardworking fellow. We see Bottom test his patience time and again but Quince never loses his temper. In fact he seems to be extremely generous in his attitude towards Bottom, probably admiring his expansive friend.

BOTTOM:

Nick Bottom is a weaver. One wonders if the fabrics he creates are as flamboyant as the man himself. He is certainly an extravagant, larger than life sort of fellow.

He seems to have great energy and enthusiasm for life. His interests are varied and while his education is limited (as we note by all his mispronunciations and misuse of words) he seems pretty confidant and considers himself to be an expert on all subjects.

He is conceited and bossy and an incredible showoff, but he manages to put together all these qualities with such charm that all the others seem to admire him greatly.

We get to see him react to some very unusual circumstances with a good-natured sense of adventure. Anyone else might respond to Titania and the fairies with resistance or fear, but Bottom approaches this with the same openness and self-assurance that he seems to have for all of life.

We note too a sense of awe and fascination when he is released from the spell and tries to make sense of what must have been a dream. For if his experiences were real, he must surely be mad!

FLUTE:

Flute is a bellows-mender. A bellows is a device for blowing air into a fire and thereby causing it to burn hotter. Flute's job was to keep the bellows in good working order.

Flute is the youngest member of this group. It is for this reason that he is selected to act the part of the girl in the play. We note his embarrassment and resistance when he protests "I have a beard coming." But we see that he ultimately does accept his assignment probably because he is so delighted to be included in this group of the older and wiser members of the community.

SNUG:

Snug is a joiner. This means that he is a furniture maker. The term joiner refers to the joining of the corners of pieces of furniture together.

Snug tells us that he is "slow of study" and there are any number of ways we can interpret this statement. Perhaps he reads slowly, or knows that he has trouble memorizing, or was one of those fellows who had problems learning in school. Whatever the case, we do note that he does a fine job when he performs in the play.

STARVELING:

Robin Starveling is a tailor, a member of the fashion industry of the time. As his name indicates, he is probably very thin, and therefore perhaps highstrung. This combination of *highstrung* and *tailor* indicates a certain *snippiness.*

It is this feminine quality of snippiness and his extreme thinness that causes him to be cast originally as Thisbe's mother. Note too that having a tailor in the company makes very good sense since he would be capable of making any costumes that might be required for the play.

TOM SNOUT:

Tom Snout is a tinker. A tinker was someone who wandered from house to house repairing pots and pans. Snout is a mature man and therefore capable of playing Pyramus' father. He is very attentive to the problems of the play and voices his concerns about the possibility of offending the aristocrats.

THE FAIRYWORLD:

We now come to the fairyworld and it is here that we must examine a whole new set of circumstances. The fairyworld is made up of immortals; beings who do not die. Perhaps this is why Titania becomes so obsessed with the boy. His mother, her closest friend, was a human and the experience of her death was no doubt a powerful blow for Titania.

Other things we note about fairies is that they can make themselves invisible as Oberon does when he wishes to overhear Helena and Demetrius' conversation. They can travel at incredible speeds; Puck tells Oberon that he will circle the globe in forty minutes to search for the love-juice and in reality, he comes back faster than that!

Fairies also know how to use magic potions and they can perfectly imitate the sound of the human voice as Puck does when he leads Lysander and Demetrius astray.

Another very important aspect of the fairy powers is control over the elements. We note that Titania and Oberon's quarrel has caused the seasons to become all confused. Since they are not in harmony, the world is out of balance. We also note that Puck, to a lessor degree perhaps, also has powers over nature. When Oberon instructs him to "overcast the night," Puck is able to darken the sky so that Lysander and Demetrius cannot find each other in the forest.

OBERON AND TITANIA:

The king and queen of fairyland are two of the most fascinating characters that Shakespeare has ever created. With them he has established a premise which seems to say that when men and women are not living together in harmony, the world is out of balance.

When they are acting in concert, Titania and Oberon create a beneficent umbrella for the world and all is well. When at odds, disharmony prevails and all nature is thrown into chaos.

Their relationship has reached a dangerous point. As with the gods of ancient Greece who were forever changing shape and seducing mortals, so Titania and Oberon have been *dabbling*. This behavior usually resulted in a great deal of trouble when the greek-god wife or husband found out about it. This is precisely what has happened with Titania and Oberon.

Their mutual infidelities have created an ever widening rift in their relationship. So much so that Titania has withdrawn all her attentions from Oberon and transferred them to a human friend.

When the friend dies in childbirth, Titania becomes obsessed with the orphaned baby. This results in a further widening of the breach between them. Oberon is plainly jealous of the attentions Titania is lavishing upon the boy and desperately wishes to get her back.

They have reached a point of mutual jealousy and suspicion that seems to escalate every time they meet. This is where they are when we are introduced to them in *Dream*.

Their relationship is out of balance and it is this balance that "Dream" is so concerned with. It is Oberon who wishes to restore the equilibrium. This is one of the driving themes of Oberon's character.

He realizes he must get the boy away from Titania in order to get her focus back where it should be; into their relationship.

He has tried unsuccessfully to get Titania to give the boy up to him as Puck tells us in his first scene. Oberon therefore hatches a plan to distract Titania's attention from the boy. He does this with the help of the love-juice.

By causing Titania to fall in love with Bottom, she lets go of her obsession with the boy long enough for Oberon to get him from her.

When he subsequently removes the love-juice's effect, equilibrium is restored and Titania is back to her right self.

OBERON:

Oberon is probably large, as fairies go, certainly larger than Puck. His age is whatever he chooses. In fact his entire appearance is what he wishes it to be.

Oberon is "passing fell and wrath." His vanity has been wounded by Titania's having placed all her affections on a child and ignoring him. Oberon is a king and like many absolute rulers in history, his need to be the center of his world is absolute. Oberon wants all of Titania's generous, feminine attentions focused back on him.

He knows he must bring about this reconciliation not only for himself, but for the sake of restoring order in the world and he must do it in such a way as order in the world and he must do it in such a way as to avoid any lasting resentments.

The solution he chooses reflects much about his nature. If Oberon were to admit responsibility for his part in their quarrel and sincerely apologize to Titania, all might be well, however his ego will not allow him to do this. Instead, he hatches his rather elaborate plan to achieve his ends. But, by his cleverness, his trickery and his ultimate kindness, he accomplishes his task.

By the conclusion of the play, this magnificent and very complex creature has not only restored balance to the world, but has done so in such a way that all affected think they have had "a most rare vision."

Also note Oberon's genuine affection for mankind. He goes out of his way to help Helena. He manages to get Helena and Demetrius together, restores Lysander and Hermia's relationship and sincerely blesses Hippolyta and Theseus' union.

He cannot be called perfect, but if more rulers were like him, our dreams would be far more pleasant.

TITANIA:

Titania is the queen of the fairies. She represents the female, nurturing side of life. She is open and generous to those she loves as we learn from Puck's description of her treatment of the young orphan boy and as we see demonstrated when she falls in love with Bottom under the influence of the love-juice.

Oberon is not currently in Titania's favor and so we get to see another side of her when she deals with him.

Oberon calls her "proud Titania." Shakespeare is using *proud* here to mean arrogant, haughty, and disdainful. And this is certainly another aspect of her character.

We also immediately note Titania's jealousy. She is quick to accuse Oberon of having had an affair with Hippolyta.

Titania is well aware that their dissension is causing horrible problems for the world but she is unwilling to part with the orphan boy as Oberon insists.

Imagine this scenario: Titania, jealous of Oberon's infidelities, has confided her emotional pain to her human friend. They become confidants and best friends. But this friend is human and dies giving birth to a baby boy.

This may be Titania's first experience with death. Members of the fairyworld are immortal and they do not die.

It is perhaps this experience, along with the rejection that she feels from Oberon's suspected affairs, that contributes to Titania's current state of mind. This is not to suggest that Titania is weepy—there is no evidence of that—but she is definitely not her normal self. And poor Oberon is at a loss to figure out how to deal with her.

Another aspect of Titania's character to note, is her strength. She is regal to her core, statuesque and elegant in her bearing. She does not *ask,* she *commands.*

PUCK:

In creating Puck, Shakespeare has combined stories of various sprites and hobgoblins dating back a thousand years.

The origin of the word *puck* is *puca* an Old English word meaning evil spirit. Over the course of time, evil was mitigated to mischievous. And in *Dream* Shakespeare has turned his Puck into a lovable scamp and that's just what he is.

He means no real harm but loves to create confusion. He is one of the first practical jokers. His attitude towards humans is summed up in one of Shakespeare's most famous lines, "lord, what fools these mortals be!"

In the course of carrying out Oberon's wishes, note that Puck is very creative and shows a great deal of initiative.

FIRST FAIRY:

First Fairy is the *advance man* for Titania. This is probably a female fairy. Her job is to make sure everything is ready for Titania wherever she goes. She is a kind of *exterior decorator.* She is fast, efficient and friendly.

ATTENDANT FAIRIES:

This crew of helpers are all tiny in size and ready and willing to assist Titania in any way they can. They are for the most part, light, sprightly, dainty, skipping, tripping beings.

PEASEBLOSSOM is a delicate little flower of a fairy, gentle and loving.

MONSIEUR COBWEB is a well-dressed dandy of a fairy, very gallant and brave. Imagine taking on a honeybee if you were that tiny!

MUSTARDSEED is tiny and tangy. He is very courteous and probably has a deep voice.

MOTH is a gorgeous fairy, able to flit anywhere silently. Expert at fanning, and terribly attracted to light.

"Here is a scroll of every man's name which is thought fit to play in our interlude…"

(Quince: Act 1 scene 2)

Cast List	abbr.*
Theseus, Duke of Athens	Th
Hippolyta, Queen of the Amazons	Hip
Egeus, Hermia's father	E
The Four Young Lovers	
Lysander	Lys
Demetrius	Dem
Hermia	Her
Helena	Hel
Peter Quince, a carpenter	Q
Nick Bottom, a weaver	B
Francis Flute, a bellows-mender	F
Tom Snout, a tinker	Sno
Robin Starveling, a tailor	St
Snug, a joiner	Snug
Oberon, King of the Fairies	O
Titania, Queen of the Fairies	T
Puck, in Oberon's service	P
In the Service of Titania	
First Fairy	FF
Peaseblossom	
Cobweb	
Moth	
Mustardseed	
Philostrate, serves the Duke	Phil

*These are the abbreviations of the character's names that we have used in the column of stage directions that we have included for those of you wanting blocking suggestions for a production of the play. [ ] Bracketed notations that appear throughout the text are interpretive hints that we've included for actors doing either a reading or a production of the play.

1

Act One · Scene 1 scene description

When the play opens, we meet Theseus, the Duke of Athens and his bride-to-be, Hippolyta. We learn that they are about to be married.

Into this scene comes Egeus, a prominent citizen of Athens, along with his daughter, Hermia, and two young men, Lysander and Demetrius. We discover that Egeus is furious because Hermia wants to marry Lysander. Egeus wants her to marry Demetrius.

Egeus asks Theseus to impose the law of Athens which says that he, as her father, has the right to "dispose of" his daughter as he chooses.

Hermia then asks the duke what the consequences would be if she refuses to follow her father's wishes. Theseus tells her that according to the law, she must either marry Demetrius, be put to death, or become a nun.

Lysander tries to convince the Duke that he is as good a candidate as Demetrius to marry Hermia and (hoping it might help his cause) tells the Duke that Demetrius used to be in love with Helena (a friend of Hermia's) and dumped her, and that Helena is now heartbroken.

The duke advises Hermia to take some time to think about her choice and to tell him what she has decided by his and Hippolyta's wedding day. Then all exit leaving Hermia and Lysander alone onstage.

Hermia (definitely her father's daughter) is furious. Lysander tells her that according to what he has read about love, their problems are pretty typical. Hermia responds sarcastically saying that they might as well just be patient then. This finally spurs Lysander into action and he suggests they escape from Athens and her laws by eloping.

They agree to meet in the woods the following night. At this point Helena enters the scene. She is miserable because she knows that Demetrius, whom she loves, is in love with Hermia.

Hermia and Lysander, trying to cheer her up, tell her that they are planning to leave town and therefore Demetrius will not see Hermia again and that they hope Helena and Demetrius will get together.

Hermia and Lysander leave. Helena, desperate for any excuse to see Demetrius, decides to go and tell him about Hermia and Lysander's plan.

Act One · Scene 1 vernacular

[enter Theseus and Hippolyta]
THESEUS:
Now fair Hippolyta, our wedding day is drawing near.

HIPPOLYTA:
In four days the moon will shine on the night of the ceremony.

THESEUS:
Hippolyta, I wooed you during battle, but I will wed you in a different way, with splendor, with festivities and with merriment.

EGEUS: [enters with Hermia, Demetrius and Lysander]
Greetings Theseus, our celebrated duke!

THESEUS:
Thank you, good Egeus. What's the news with you?

EGEUS:
I am very annoyed and come to you with a complaint about my child, my daughter, Hermia. Step forward, Demetrius. My noble lord, this man has my consent to marry her. Step forward, Lysander. And, my gracious duke, this man has bewitched my child; stolen my daughter's heart, and turned her obedience—which she owes to me—into stubborn disobedience. And, my gracious duke, if she will not consent to marry Demetrius, I beg you to impose the old law of Athens which says that since she is mine, I may marry her to whom I choose, which shall be to this gentleman or, if she refuse, to have her put to death, according to our laws.

THESEUS:
What do you say Hermia? Demetrius is a worthy gentleman.

HERMIA:
So is Lysander.

Act One · Scene 1 **original abridged**	Act One · Scene 1 **stage directions**

[enter Theseus and Hippolyta]

THESEUS:
Now fair Hippolyta, our nuptial
hour draws on apace.

(enter from USL together, Hip L of Th, cross DLC during this conversation)

HIPPOLYTA:
Four days, and then the moon shall
behold the night of our solemnities.

THESEUS:
Hippolyta, I wooed thee with my sword,
but I will wed thee in another key,
with pomp, with triumph, and with
reveling.

(taking her hands)

EGEUS: *[enters with Hermia, Demetrius and Lysander]*
Happy be Theseus, our renowned Duke!

(interrupting this moment, enter from SR and cross to to DRC with Dem, Her and Lys stopping R and slightly behind E)

THESEUS:
Thanks, good Egeus. What's the news
with thee?

EGEUS: *[angrily]*
Full of vexation come I, with
complaint against my child, my
daughter Hermia. Stand forth
Demetrius. My Noble Lord, this man
hath my consent to marry her. Stand
forth Lysander. And my gracious
Duke, this man hath bewitched my
child: filched my daughter's heart;
turned her obedience—which is due
to me—to stubborn harshness. And,
my gracious Duke, will she not consent
to marry with Demetrius, I beg the
ancient privilege of Athens; as she
is mine, I may dispose of her; which
shall be either to this gentleman
or to her death, according to our
law.

(Dem takes one step DS into view of Th)
(Lys does the same)

(Her steps forward)

THESEUS:
What say you Hermia? Demetrius is
a worthy gentleman.

HERMIA:
So is Lysander.

(summoning her courage)

THESEUS:
Yes he is. But lacking your father's
blessing, the other must be thought
the worthier.

HERMIA:
I wish my father could see with my
eyes!

THESEUS:
Better yet, your eyes should see with
his judgement.

HERMIA:
I beg your grace to pardon me. I don't
know what has made me so bold, but let
me ask your grace, what is the worst
that can happen to me if I refuse to
marry Demetrius?

THESEUS:
Either to be put to death, or to give
up forever the company of men. Therefore
fair Hermia, ask yourself what you really
want. Could you stand the life of a
nun?

HERMIA:
I would, my lord, before I'd give up
my virginity to him!

THESEUS:
Take some time to think; and by the
next new moon—which is the wedding
day for my love and me—on that day
either be ready to die for disobeying
your father; or else to marry Demetrius; or
to take the vows of a nun.

DEMETRIUS:
Give in, sweet Hermia, and Lysander,
give up!

LYSANDER:
You've got her father's love
Demetrius; let me have Hermia's.
Marry him!

Act One · Scene 1 **original abridged**	Act One · Scene 1 **stage directions**
THESEUS: In himself he is. But wanting your father's voice, the other must be held the worthier.	
HERMIA: I would my father looked but with my eyes!	*(apologizing for her boldness, but determined to be heard)*
THESEUS: Rather, your eyes must with his judgement look.	
HERMIA: I do entreat your Grace to pardon me. I know not by what power I am made bold, but I beseech your Grace, that I may know the worst that may befall me in this case if I refuse to wed Demetrius.	*(crossing in a little More to Th)*
THESEUS: Either to die the death, or to abjure forever the society of men. Therefore fair Hermia, question your desires. Can you endure the livery of a nun?	*(crossing in a bit to Her)*
HERMIA: So will I my Lord, ere I will yield my virgin patent up unto him!	*(points to Dem)*
THESEUS: Take time to pause; and by the next new moon—the sealing day betwixt my love and me—upon that day either prepare to die, for disobedience to your father's will; or else to wed Demetrius; or to protest for single life.	
DEMETRIUS: Relent, sweet Hermia; and Lysander, yield.	*(cross down to R of Her then turning to Lys)*
LYSANDER: You have her father's love Demetrius; let me have Hermia's. You marry him!	*(cross to R of Dem)*

Act One • Scene 1   vernacular

EGEUS:
Contemptuous Lysander! it's true, he
does have my love; and all the rights
I have in her, I give to Demetrius.

LYSANDER: *[making his stand]*
I am, my lord, from as good a family
as he, as well off; my love is stronger
than his; and—what's more—beautiful
Hermia loves me. Demetrius wooed Helena
and won her; and she—sweet lady—dotes,
devoutly dotes, dotes devotedly, on
this fickle man.

THESEUS:
I must admit that I have heard that.
Demetrius, come; and come Egeus; you
shall go with me. As for you, pretty
Hermia, adapt your desires to your
father's wishes; or else the law of
Athens requires your death or your vow
to be a nun. Come, Hippolyta.

EGEUS:
We'll follow you. *[all exit except Hermia
and Lysander]*

LYSANDER: *[trying to console Hermia]*
How are you my love?

HERMIA:
Oh hell! To be forced to choose love
through someone else's eyes.

LYSANDER:
Oh my! According to everything I've
ever read, the path of true love is
never smooth.

HERMIA: *[sarcastically]*
Then we must learn to accept our
suffering with patience.

LYSANDER:
I see what you mean; then listen to
me, Hermia. I have a widow aunt who's
very rich, and has no children. Her
house is far from Athens and she thinks

EGEUS:
Scornful Lysander! true, he hath
my love; and all my right of her,
I do estate unto Demetrius.

LYSANDER: *[making his stand]*
I am, my Lord, as well derived as
he, as well possessed; my love is
more than his; and—which is more—
I am beloved of beauteous Hermia.
Demetrius made love to Helena and
won her soul; and she—sweet lady—
dotes, devoutly dotes, dotes in
idolatry, upon this inconstant man.

THESEUS:
I must confess that I have heard
so much. Demetrius, come; and come
Egeus; you shall go with me. For
you, fair Hermia, fit your fancies
to your father's will; or else the
law of Athens yields you up to death,
or to a vow of single life. Come,
my Hippolyta.

EGEUS:
We follow you. *[all exit except Hermia
and Lysander]*

LYSANDER: *[trying to console Hermia]*
How now my love?

HERMIA: *[very upset]*
O hell! To choose love by another's
eye.

LYSANDER:
Ay me! for aught that I could ever
read, the course of true love never
did run smooth.

HERMIA: *[sarcastically]*
Then let us teach our trial patience.

LYSANDER: *[getting the message]*
A good persuasion; therefore, hear
me Hermia. I have a widow aunt of
great revenue, and she hath no child;
from Athens is her house removed;

*(Th, Hip, Dem and Eg
exit UL)*

(cross to Her)

of me as her only son. There, gentle
Hermia, I can marry you, and, being
so far away, the laws of Athens cannot
apply to us. If you love me, then sneak
out of your father's house tomorrow
night, and in the woods, three miles
out of town, I will be waiting for you.

HERMIA:
My good Lysander! I swear to you, that
at the place you told me to, tomorrow
I will meet with you.

LYSANDER:
Look, here comes Helena. *[Helena
enters]*

HERMIA:
Good day, fair Helena! Where are you
off to?

HELENA:
You call me fair? Take back that fair.
Demetrius loves your fair; oh, yours
is a happy fair! Sickness is catching;
oh, if only your looks were too! Then
I would catch them, fair Hermia, from
you. Oh, teach me how you look and with
what charms you have won over Demetrius'
heart.

HERMIA:
I frown at him, yet he loves me still.

HELENA:
Oh, I wish your frowns could teach my
smiles that skill!

HERMIA:
The more I hate him, the more he follows
me.

HELENA:
The more I love him, the more he hates
me.

HERMIA:
His stupidity, Helena, is no fault of
mine.

and she respects me as her only son.
There, gentle Hermia, may I marry
thee, and to that place the sharp
Athenian law cannot pursue us. If
thou lovest me, then steal forth
thy father's house tomorrow night;
and in the wood, a league without
the town, there will I stay for thee.

HERMIA:
My good Lysander! I swear to thee,
in that same place thou hast appointed
me, tomorrow truly will I meet with
thee.

LYSANDER:
Look, here comes Helena. *[Helena
enters]*

HERMIA:
Godspeed fair Helena! Whither away?

HELENA:
Call you me fair? That fair again
unsay. Demetrius loves your fair;
O happy fair! Sickness is catching;
O, were favor so! Yours would I catch,
fair Hermia, ere I go. O, teach me
how you look, and with what art you
sway the motion of Demetrius' heart.

HERMIA:
I frown upon him, yet he loves me
still.

HELENA:
O that your frowns would teach my
smiles such skill!

HERMIA:
The more I hate, the more he follows
me.

HELENA:
The more I love, the more he hateth
me.

HERMIA:
His folly, Helena, is no fault of
mine.

*(Lys and Her move in to
kiss but are interrupted
by Hel's loud sigh)*
*(Hel enters from SR,
sighing audibly, sees them,
crosses DSR, sighing louder,
she sits on stool)*
*(crossing to L of Hel,
she kneels facing her)*

(playing for sympathy)

(responding sympathetically)

Act One · Scene 1   **vernacular**

HELENA:
It's the fault of your beauty; I wish
that fault were mine!

HERMIA:
Don't worry, he will never again see
my face. Lysander and I are going to
escape from this place.

LYSANDER:
Helen, to you our secret we will reveal.
Tomorrow night, away from Athens we
have planned to steal.

HERMIA:
In the woods, where you and I often
did retreat, there my Lysander and myself
will meet. Farewell, sweet playmate,
pray for us, and may good luck bring
you your Demetrius.

LYSANDER:
Helena, adieu: as much as you adore
him, may Demetrius adore you!
[Hermia and Lysander exit]

HELENA:
Why are some people so much happier
than others? Throughout Athens I am
thought as fair as she. But so what!
Demetrius doesn't think so; he can't
see what everyone else already knows.
And, just as he foolishly dotes on
Hermia, so I foolishly dote on him.
Things ordinary, even awful, having
no value, love can transform to beauty
and worth. Before Demetrius looked into
Hermia's eyes, he snowed me and swore
that he was only mine; but when the
snow job felt a little of Hermia's heat,
it all dissolved and he did a retreat.
I will go tell him of fair Hermia's
intended flight; then he will follow
her tomorrow night. If I get any thanks
for my news, it's still a high price
to pay. But I'm willing to suffer the
pain, if only to see his face once again.
[she exits]

HELENA:
None but your beauty; would that
fault were mine!

HERMIA:
Take comfort, he no more shall see
my face; Lysander and myself will
fly this place.

LYSANDER:
Helen, to you our minds we will
reveal. Tomorrow night, from Athens
we have devised to steal.

HERMIA:
In the wood, where you and I were
wont to retreat, there my Lysander
and myself shall meet. Farewell,
sweet playfellow, pray thou for us,
and good luck grant thee thy
Demetrius!

LYSANDER:
Helena, adieu: as you on him,
Demetrius dote on you! *[Hermia and
Lysander exit]*

HELENA:
How happy some o'er other some can
be! Through Athens I am thought as
fair as she. But what of that?
Demetrius thinks not so; he will
not know what all but he do know.
And as he errs, doting on Hermia's
eyes, so I, admiring of his qualities.
Things base and vile, holding no
quantity, love can transpose to form
and dignity. Ere Demetrius looked
on Hermia's eyne, he hailed down
oaths that he was only mine; but
when this hail some heat from Hermia
felt, so he dissolved, and showers
of oaths did melt. I will go tell
him of fair Hermia's flight: then
to the wood will he tomorrow night,
pursue her. And for this intelligence
if I have thanks, it is a dear
expense. But herein mean I to enrich
my pain, to have his sight thither
and back again. *[she exits]*

*(crossing down to R of
Hel, he kneels)*

(Her and Lys exit SR)

(see note on monologues*)
(very miserable and depressed)

(suddenly getting a new idea)

(Hel exits SR)

Act One • Scene 2   scene description

This scene introduces the workmen of Athens. They have gathered together to prepare a little play to celebrate the Duke and Duchess' wedding day.

Quince tries to get things underway and at every step is thwarted by Bottom who is a somewhat pompous, pretentious, but very lovable *ass*.

They finally get the various parts distributed and decide to meet the next night outside of town to rehearse.

Act One • Scene 2   vernacular

[enter Quince, Snug, Bottom, Flute, Snout and Starveling]

QUINCE:
Is the whole company here?

BOTTOM: *[interrupting]*
It would be best for you to call them generally, one by one, according to your list.

QUINCE:
Here is the list of everyone's name who is thought to be suitable to act in our play to be given for the Duke and Duchess on his wedding day at night.

BOTTOM: *[interrupting again]*
First, good Peter Quince, tell us what the play deals with, then read the names of the actors.

QUINCE:
Indeed, our play is "The most sorrowful comedy and most cruel death of Pyramus and Thisbe."

BOTTOM:
A very good piece of work, I assure you. Now, good Peter Quince, call your actors according to the list.
Men, give him room.

QUINCE: *[reading from his list]*
Answer as I call you. Nick Bottom, the weaver.

BOTTOM:
Here. Which part am I down for?

QUINCE:
You, Nick Bottom, are down for Pyramus.

BOTTOM:
What is Pyramus, a lover or a tyrant?

QUINCE:
A lover who kills himself for love.

Act One • Scene 2 **original abridged**	Act One • Scene 2 **stage directions**

[enter Quince, Snug, Bottom, Flute, Snout and Starveling]

(enter from DR in a clump behind Q who has the script they all want to see—there should be appropriate adlibs*)
(Q stops LC, "sh, sh's" to quiet them down)

QUINCE:
Is all our company here?

BOTTOM: *[interrupting]*
You were best to call them generally, man by man, according to the scrip.

QUINCE:
Here is the scroll of every man's name, which is thought fit to play in our interlude before the Duke and the Duchess, on his wedding day at night.

(holding up paper)

BOTTOM: *[interrupting again]*
First, good Peter Quince, say what the play treats on; then read the names of the actors.

QUINCE:
Marry, our play is—"The most lamentable comedy and most cruel death of Pyramus and Thisbe."

(reading from the cover of his script)

BOTTOM:
A very good piece of work I assure you. Now good Peter Quince, call forth your actors by the scroll. Masters, spread yourselves.

(Q remains standing, B sits on DL stool, others sit on ground in semicircle around Q)

QUINCE: *[reading from his list]*
Answer as I call you. Nick Bottom the weaver.

BOTTOM:
Ready. Name what part I am for.

(B stands)

QUINCE:
You Nick Bottom, are set down for Pyramus.

BOTTOM:
What is Pyramus, a lover or a tyrant?

QUINCE:
A lover that kills himself for love.

BOTTOM:
My greatest wish is to play a tyrant.
I could play Hercules excellently;
    The raging rocks
    And shivering shocks
    Shall break the locks
    of prison gates.
That was lofty. Now name the rest of
the players.

QUINCE:
Francis Flute, the bellows-mender.

FLUTE:
Here, Peter Quince.

QUINCE:
Flute, you must take the part of Thisbe.

FLUTE:
What is Thisbe—a wandering knight?

QUINCE:
It is the lady that Pyramus loves.

FLUTE:
No, really, don't make me play a woman;
I started shaving—last week.

QUINCE:
That doesn't matter, you will play it
in a mask, and you may speak in a tiny
voice .

BOTTOM:
If I could wear a mask, I could play
Thisbe too. I'll speak in a teeny, tiny,
little voice; *[he pretends to be Pyramus]*
"Thisne, Thisne!" *[he pretends to be
Thisbe]* "Ah Pyramus, my lover dear!"

QUINCE:
No no, you must play Pyramus, and Flute,
you Thisbe.

BOTTOM:
Oh well, go on.

BOTTOM:
My chief humor is for a tyrant: I
could play Ercles rarely;
    The raging rocks
    And shivering shocks
    Shall break the locks
    of prison gates.
This was lofty! Now name the rest
of the players.

(overacting outrageously in his efforts to demonstrate this speech)

(B sits on the stool)

QUINCE:
Francis Flute, the bellows-mender.

FLUTE:
Here, Peter Quince.

(F stands)

QUINCE:
Flute, you must take Thisbe on you.

FLUTE:
What is Thisbe—a wand'ring knight?

QUINCE:
It is the lady that Pyramus must
love.

FLUTE:
Nay faith, let not me play a woman;
I have a beard—coming.

QUINCE:
That's all one; you shall play it
in a mask, and you may speak as small
as you will.

BOTTOM:
An I may hide my face, let me play
Thisbe too. I'll speak in a monstrous
little voice; *[as Pyramus]* "Thisne,
Thisne!" *[as Thisbe]* "Ah Pyramus,
my lover dear!"

(gets up and pushes F aside, crosses to Q, F sits)

QUINCE:
No no, you must play Pyramus, and
Flute, you Thisbe.

BOTTOM:
Well, proceed.

(B sits on stool)

QUINCE:
Robin Starveling, the tailor.

STARVELING:
Here, Peter Quince.

QUINCE:
Robin Starveling, you must play
Thisbe's mother. Tom Snout, the
tinker.

SNOUT:
Here, Peter Quince.

QUINCE:
You, Pyramus' father; myself,
Thisbe's father; Snug, the
furniture-maker, you will play the lion.

SNUG:
Do you have the lion's part written
out? I beg you, if you do give it to
me, because I'm a slow study.

QUINCE:
You can just ad lib it, it's only
roaring.

BOTTOM:
Let me play the lion too. It will
do everyone good to hear me. The
duke will even say, "Let him roar
again; let him roar again!"

QUINCE:
If you did too much, you would scare
the Duchess and the ladies and make
them shriek, and that would be enough
to get us all hanged.

BOTTOM:
I will change my voice so that I will
roar as gently as a dove.

QUINCE:
You can play no part but Pyramus!—
for Pyramus is a handsome man; a most
lovely, gentleman-like man; therefore
you must play Pyramus.

Act One · Scene 2 **original abridged**	Act One · Scene 2 **stage directions**
QUINCE: Robin Starveling, the tailor.	
STARVELING: Here, Peter Quince.	*(St stands)*
QUINCE: Robin Starveling, you must play Thisbe's mother. Tom Snout, the tinker.	*(St nods and sits)*
SNOUT: Here, Peter Quince.	*(Sno stands)*
QUINCE: You, Pyramus' father; myself, Thisbe's father; Snug, the joiner, you, the lion's part.	*(Sno sits)*
SNUG: Have you the lion's part written? Pray you, if it be, give it me, for I am slow of study.	*(Snug rises, crosses to Q)*
QUINCE: You may do it extempore, for it is nothing but roaring.	
BOTTOM: Let me play the lion too. It will do any man's heart good to hear me. I will make the Duke say, "Let him roar again; let him roar again!"	*(B rises, crosses to Q, Snug sits)* *(B gives a giant roar)*
QUINCE: If you should do it too terribly, you would fright the Duchess and the ladies, that they would shriek; and that were enough to hang us all.	
BOTTOM: But I will aggravate my voice so, that I will roar as gently as a dove.	*(B does a very gently roar)*
QUINCE: You can play no part but Pyramus!— for Pyramus is a sweet-faced man; a most lovely, gentleman-like man; therefore you must play Pyramus.	*(briefly losing his cool)* *(trying to win him with flattery)*

Act One • Scene 2   vernacular

BOTTOM:
Well, I'll do it.

QUINCE:
Men, here are your parts:
and I beg you, implore you, and
desire you, to memorize them
by tomorrow night, and to meet me in
the woods near the palace, a mile outside
of town, when the moon comes up—we
will rehearse there. I beg you, don't
fail me.

BOTTOM:
We'll be there. Adieu. *[they exit]*

Act Two • Scene 1   scene description

We now meet the members of the fairy world. It is evening and Puck and one of Titania's fairies meet in the woods and they reveal to each other (and of course to the audience) that their respective bosses are having a feud over a little orphan boy who is in Titania's care and whom Oberon wants in his entourage.

Just as we learn of their anger towards each other, Oberon and Titania show up. Immediately they start in on each other, Oberon demanding the boy and Titania refusing him.

We discover that due to their quarreling, the seasons have all gone awry and the world is in a state of confusion.

Oberon tells Titania that if she will give him the boy, all will be well again. She refuses once more and leaves.

Oberon wants revenge and remembers a flower that he once saw hit by one of Cupid's arrows. The juice of this flower, when squeezed into the eyes of someone asleep, has the power to make them fall in love with the first living thing they see when they awake.

Oberon sends Puck to get the flower and tells the audience that he plans to squeeze it into Titania's eyes and hopes that she will awaken when some awful creature is nearby. While she is distracted with this creature, he intends to make her give up

Act Two • Scene 1   vernacular

[enter fairy and Puck from separate entrances]
PUCK:
What's up, spirit? Where you off to?

FAIRY:
Off to here, off to there, I am off
to everywhere; and I serve the Fairy
Queen. Farewell, I must prepare, the
Queen is soon coming here.

PUCK:
The King too will be coming here tonight;
be sure the Queen stays out of his sight.
Oberon is full of rage, because of the
boy—stolen from an Indian king—that
she keeps as her page. Jealous Oberon
wants the child, but she will not part
with him. She crowns him with flowers
and devotes herself to him. And now
whenever they meet, they quarrel.

FAIRY:
If I'm not mistaken, you are that shrewd
and rascally sprite called Robin
Goodfellow, Are you, "Sweet Puck," are
you?

Act One · Scene 2 **original abridged**

BOTTOM:
Well, I will undertake it.

QUINCE:
Masters, here are your parts:
and I am to entreat you,
request you, and desire you,
to con them by tomorrow night, and
meet me in the palace wood, a mile
without the town, by moonlight—there
we will rehearse. I pray you, fail
me not.

BOTTOM:
We will meet. Adieu. *[they exit]*

Act One · Scene 2 **stage directions**

(taking the bait)

(hands out papers to all)

(ad libs of "goodnight," "adieu,"
etc. as they all exit in various
directions except UC and DR)*

Act Two · Scene 1 **original abridged**

*[enter Fairy and Puck from separate
entrances]*
PUCK:
How now, spirit! Whither wander you?

FIRST FAIRY:
Over hill, over dale, I do wander
everywhere; and I serve the Fairy
Queen. Farewell, I'll be gone, our
Queen comes here anon.

PUCK:
The King doth keep his revels here
tonight; take heed the Queen come
not within his sight. Oberon is
passing fell and wrath, because she,
as her attendant, hath a lovely boy
stolen from an Indian king—and
jealous Oberon would have the child.
But she withholds the boy, crowns him
with flowers, and makes him all her
joy. And now they never meet but they
do square.

FIRST FAIRY:
Either I mistake, or else you are
that shrewd and knavish sprite called
Robin Goodfellow. Are not you he?
"Sweet Puck,"—are not you he?

Act Two · Scene 1 **stage directions**

*(P enters UC, looking for
mischief, as FF enters DR
blowing bubbles* and saying
"OOOH," P hides behind platform, as FF comes near, P
pops up yelling and frightens
her, she jumps and recovers)*
*(continues blowing bubbles,
preparing the spot for T,
not having time for small
talk)*

(perching on the platform)

*(having blown bubbles all
around, stops and crosses
to P)*

Act Two · Scene 1   scene description

Cont.

the orphan boy. He then will remove the spell, which he can do with another flower.

At this moment Demetrius comes on with Helena in hot pursuit. Oberon makes himself invisible and stays to listen to their conversation.

Demetrius tells Helena that he does not love her and that she should stop following him. She tells him that she can't help it because he attracts her so greatly. Demetrius tries to run off and Helena runs after him.

Oberon decides to help Helena. He sends Puck (who has by now returned with the magic flower) off with some of the love-juice to find the man wearing Athenian clothing and to squeeze some juice in his eyes at a time when the next thing he will see will be Helena. Oberon himself is off to find Titania.

Act Two · Scene 1   vernacular

PUCK:
Yup, you're right; I'm that cheerful fellow of the night. But stand back, fairy. Here comes Oberon.

FAIRY:
And here comes my mistress:—I wish that he were gone!

OBERON:
Ill met by moonlight, proud Titania.

TITANIA:
Oberon!

OBERON:
Stay!

TITANIA:
Why are you here? *[not waiting for an answer]* Never since the middle of summer, have my fairies gathered on the hill, in the dale, the forest or the mead, but your quarreling has disrupted our pastimes. This has caused the seasons to go awry: the spring, the summer, autumn and winter are all confused and the stunned world cannot tell which is which. This evil is the result of our quarreling; we are the cause!

OBERON:
If you wish to change things, it's within your power. Why does Titania cross Oberon? I only want the little orphan boy.

TITANIA:
Set your heart at rest—the whole of Fairy Land couldn't buy the child from me. His mother was a member of my order. But, being human, she died in childbirth, and for her sake I am bringing up her boy, and for her sake I will not part with him.

OBERON:
Give me the boy!

Act Two · Scene 1 **original abridged**	Act Two · Scene 1 **stage directions**
PUCK: Thou speakest aright; I am that merry wonderer of the night. But room, fairy, here comes Oberon.	*(O enters UL)*
FIRST FAIRY: And here my mistress:—would that he were gone!	*(T enters DR with her fairies following)* *(FF joins T's group, P crosses UL of O and listens)*
OBERON: Ill met by moonlight, proud Titania.	*(cross C)*
TITANIA: Oberon!	*(turns to leave DR)*
OBERON: Tarry!	
TITANIA: Why art thou here? *[not waiting for an answer]* Never since the middle summer's spring, met we on hill, in dale, forest, or mead, but with thy brawls thou hast disturbed our sport. Therefore, the seasons alter: the spring, the summer, autumn, and winter change their wonted liveries, and the mazed world now knows not which is which. And this evil comes from our dissension; we are their parents and original.	*(turning back to him and crosses to O)* *(T fairies kneel and crouch near DR entrance and watch during all this)*
OBERON: Do you amend it then; it lies in you? Why should Titania cross her Oberon? I do but beg a little changeling boy.	*(trying to be rational with T)*
TITANIA: Set your heart at rest—the Fairy Land buys not the child of me! His mother was a vot'ress of my order. But she, being mortal, of that boy did die; and for her sake, do I rear up her boy; and for her sake, I will not part with him.	
OBERON: Give me that boy!	*(insistently)*

Act Two • Scene 1   vernacular

TITANIA:
Not for your fairy kingdom. Fairies,
away. *[Titania and her fairies exit]*

OBERON:
Well, go. I will torment you for this
insult. Gentle Puck, come here. Once
when I was sitting on a rock, I saw
Cupid shoot his love-arrow from his
bow. I noticed where Cupid's arrow fell.
It fell on a little flower which young
girls call "love-in-idleness."

PUCK:
I remember.

OBERON:
Bring me that flower. When the juice
of it is placed on the eyelids of someone
asleep, it will cause that man or woman
to dote on the next living thing it
sees.

PUCK:
I'll search the world in forty minutes.

OBERON:
When I have this juice, I'll keep watch
till Titania is asleep and then drop
it in her eyes. The next thing she sees
when she awakes—whether it's a lion,
bear, or an ape—she will pursue it
with all her heart. And before I remove
this charm from her eyes—which I can
do with another flower—I'll make her
give me the boy. But who is coming?
I'll make myself invisible and hear
their conversation.

[enter Demetrius with Helena following]
DEMETRIUS:
I don't love you, therefore do not pursue
me. Where is Lysander and lovely Hermia?
You told me they had snuck off into
these woods. Away, get lost, quit
following me.

Act Two · Scene 1 **original abridged**	Act Two · Scene 1 **stage directions**

TITANIA:
Not for thy fairy kingdom. Fairies,
away. *[Titania and her fairies exit]*

(defiantly)
(T exits DR, fairies follow)

OBERON:
Well, go thy way. I will torment
thee for this injury. My gentle Puck,
come hither. Once I sat upon a
promentory and saw Cupid loose his
love-shaft from his bow. Marked I
where the bolt of Cupid fell. It
fell upon a little flower; maidens
call it "love-in-idleness."

(looking off DR after T)

(P crosses to L of O)

PUCK:
I remember.

OBERON:
Fetch me that flower. The juice of it,
on sleeping eyelids laid, will make
man or woman madly dote upon the
next live creature that it sees.

PUCK:
I'll round the earth in forty minutes.

(P runs off DL)

OBERON:
Having this juice, I'll watch Titania
when she is asleep and drop the liquor
of it in her eyes. The next thing
she waking looks upon—be it on
lion, bear, or on ape—she shall
pursue it with the soul of love.
And ere I take this charm from off
her sight—as I can take it with
another herb—I'll make her render
up her page to me. But who comes
here? I am invisible!—and I will
overhear their conference.

(see note on monologues)*

(starts up to platform, lies down across it, hears voices, snaps his fingers to make himself invisible)*

[enter Demetrius with Helena following him]
DEMETRIUS:
I love thee not, therefore pursue
me not. Where is Lysander and fair
Hermia? Thou told'st me they were
stol'n unto this wood. Hence, get
thee gone, and follow me no more.

(enter from UR speaking as they come on)

(Dem crossing C, looking)
(turning back to Hel, starting off DL)

Act Two · Scene 1	vernacular

HELENA:
You attract me. Stop being so
attractive and I'll stop following
you.

DEMETRIUS:
Do I entice you? Do I tell you you're
pretty? Or rather have I not simply
told you that I do not and I cannot
love you?

HELENA:
And even for that I love you more.

DEMETRIUS:
I get sick when I see you.

HELENA:
And I get sick when I don't see you.

DEMETRIUS:
I'll run away and hide and leave you
at the mercy of wild beasts.

HELENA:
The wildest is not as hard-hearted as
you. Run! Only let me follow you.

DEMETRIUS:
I won't stay. Let me go!

HELENA:
Damn, Demetrius! Your treatment of me
is a scandal to all women. *[he exits]*
We can't fight for love the way men
do; we should be wooed and were not
made to woo. *[she follows Demetrius]*

OBERON:
Farewell, nymph. Before he leaves this
grove, he will seek your love. *[enter
Puck]* Have you got the flower?

Act Two · Scene 1 **original abridged**	Act Two · Scene 1 **stage directions**
HELENA: You draw me. Leave you your power to draw, and I shall have no power to follow you.	*(right on his heels, Hel follows him DL)*
DEMETRIUS: Do I entice you? Do I speak you fair? Or rather, do I not in plainest truth tell you—I do not, nor I cannot love you?	*(with exaggerated patience)*
HELENA: And even for that do I love you the more.	
DEMETRIUS: I am sick when I do look on thee.	*(deliberately)*
HELENA: And I am sick when I look not on you.	*(undeterred)*
DEMETRIUS: I'll run from thee and hide me and leave thee to the mercy of wild beasts.	
HELENA: The wildest hath not such a heart as you. Run! Only give me leave to follow you.	*(grabbing his right arm as he starts to move DL)*
DEMETRIUS: I will not stay. Let me go!	*(after some struggle, Dem breaks free)*
HELENA: Fie, Demetrius! Your wrongs do set a scandal on my sex. *[he exits]* We cannot fight for love, as men may do; we should be wooed, and were not made to woo. *[she follows Demetrius]*	*(exits DL)* *(Hel exits DL)*
OBERON: Fare thee well, nymph. Ere he leave this grove, he shall seek thy love. *[enter Puck]* Hast thou the flower?	*(snaps fingers to become visible and steps off platform, crosses C as P enters from UC and crosses to O)*

Act Two · Scene 1   vernacular

PUCK:
Yup, there it is.

OBERON:
I know where Titania sleeps for part
of the night, and I'll apply the juice
of this to her eyes. You take some of
it, and search through the woods, a
sweet Athenian lady is in love with
a disdainful young man. Put some in
his eyes; but do it when the next thing
he sees will be the lady. You will know
the man by the Athenian clothing he
has on.

PUCK:
Don't worry, my lord, your servant will
do it. *[they exit]*

Act Two · Scene 2   scene description

In this scene, we find ourselves in the spot where Titania sleeps. She asks her fairies to sing her a lullaby to put her to sleep, they do so and then leave.

At this point Oberon comes on and applies the love-juice to Titania's eyes and then he leaves.

Lysander and Hermia enter. Both are tired and Lysander admits that he is lost and suggests that they sleep where they are and wait for daylight before continuing. Hermia agrees but insists that Lysander sleep far enough away from her to preserve her sense of modesty. He moves away and they both fall asleep.

Puck, who has been looking through the woods for the man dressed in Athenian clothing, comes on and sees Lysander and thinks he has found his man. He applies the love-juice to Lysander's eyes and exits.

Demetrius then enters with Helena close behind. He manages to break free of her and runs off. Helena, exhausted sits down to rest right near where Lysander has fallen asleep. She notices him, wakes him and under the power of the love-juice, he instantly falls madly in love her. Helena thinks Lysander is making fun of her and she walks off and Lysander follows her.

Act Two · Scene 2   vernacular

[enter Titania and her fairies]
TITANIA:
Come, sing me to sleep, and let me rest.

[the fairies sing]
Lulla, lulla, lullaby, lulla, lulla,
lullaby.
        Never harm
        Nor spell or charm
        Come to our lovely lady here.
        So good night, with lullaby.
[Titania sleeps, fairies exit]

*[Oberon enters and puts the juice in
Titania's eye]*
OBERON:
        What thou seest when thou dost wake,
        Love and languish for his sake;
        When thou wak'st, it is thy dear;
        Wake, when some vile thing is near.
[he exits]
[enter Lysander and Hermia]

Act Two · Scene 1 **original abridged**

PUCK:
Ay, there it is.

OBERON:
I know where sleeps Titania sometime
of the night, and with the juice
of this I'll streak her eyes. Take
thou some of it, and seek through
this grove, a sweet Athenian lady
is in love with a disdainful youth.
Anoint his eyes; but do it when the
next thing he espies may be the lady.
Thou shalt know the man by the
Athenian garments he hath on.

PUCK:
Fear not my lord, your servant shall
do so. *[they exit]*

Act Two · Scene 1 **stage directions**

(handing O the flower)

*(plucks off a petal
and gives it to P, and
indicates DL where Hel and
Dem have gone)*

(P exits DL, O exits L)

Act Two · Scene 2 **original abridged**

[enter Titania and her fairies]
TITANIA:
Come, sing me now asleep, and let
me rest.

[the fairies sing]
Lulla, lulla, lullaby, lulla, lulla,
lullaby.
    Never harm,
    Nor spell, nor charm,
    Come our lovely lady nigh,
    So good night with lullaby.
[Titania sleeps, fairies exit]

*[Oberon enters and puts the juice
in Titania's eyes]*
OBERON:
    What thou seest when thou dost wake,
    Love and languish for his sake;
    When thou wak'st, it is thy dear;
    Wake, when some vile thing is near.
    [he exits]

[enter Lysander and Hermia]

Act Two · Scene 2 **stage directions**

(enter UL)

*(T crosses to platform
and lies down)*

*(fairies surround her and
sing*)*

(fairies exit UR)

*(O enters UL, crosses
to T, applies love-juice)*
(this is a sort of chant)

(O exits DL)

*(enter from UL, Lys first, referring to map
looks around, come C, Her follows*

Act Two · Scene 2 **scene description**	Act Two · Scene 2 **vernacular**

Cont.

Hermia, who has had a bad dream, wakes up frightened and calls out for Lysander. After a few fruitless tries to locate him, she realizes that he is gone and she goes off to find out what has happened to him.

LYSANDER:
Dear love, I've lost our way. We'll rest Hermia, and wait for the comfort of the day.

HERMIA:
No, good Lysander, for my sake, my dear, lie further off. Do not lie so near.

LYSANDER:
Oh!

HERMIA:
Gentle friend, for love and courtesy, lie further away—for modesty.

LYSANDER:
Here is my bed. Let sleep give you a good rest! *[they both sleep]*

[enter puck]
PUCK:
Through the forest I have gone, but as for Athenians, I've found none. *[he sees Lysander]* Who is this? Clothing of Athens he wears. This is he! Churl, upon your eyes I throw all the power this charm can bestow. So awake, when I am gone; for now I must go to Oberon. *[he exits]*

[enter Demetrius with Helena running after him]
HELENA:
Stop, sweet Demetrius.

DEMETRIUS:
I beg you, go away, and don't bother me.

and stops L of Lys, they look around, it's dark, scary, an owl hoots,* Her screams, runs into Lys arms, fear changes to an awareness of each other, it's a little awkward, Lys speaks)

LYSANDER:
Fair love, I have forgot our way.
We'll rest us, Hermia, and wait for
the comfort of the day.

(Her lies down L of C, Lys lies R of C)

HERMIA:
Nay, good Lysander, for my sake,
my dear, lie further off. Do not
lie so near.

LYSANDER:
O!

(Lys moves a little R)

HERMIA:
Gentle friend, for love and courtesy,
lie further off—in human modesty.

LYSANDER:
Here is my bed. Sleep give thee all
her rest! *[they both sleep]*

(he moves to DR)

[enter Puck]
PUCK:
Through the forest have I gone, but
Athenian found I none. *[he sees
Lysander]* Who is here? Weeds of Athens
he doth wear. This is he! Churl,
upon thy eyes I throw all the power
this charm doth owe. So awake, when
I am gone; for I must now to Oberon.
[he exits]

*(enter from UL speaking
as he crosses DR and sees
Lys)*

(applies juice to Lys eyes)

(exits DR)

*[enter Demetrius and Helena running
after him]*
HELENA:
Stay, sweet Demetrius.

*(Dem enters from DL with Hel in
hot pursuit, they get to DRC
between Her and Lys, not noticing
them, Hel grabbing for Dem)*

DEMETRIUS:
I charge thee, hence, and do not
haunt me thus.

*(breaks free, turns to
Hel)*

Act Two • Scene 2   **vernacular**

HELENA:
Oh, will you leave me? Don't.

DEMETRIUS:
Remain at your peril; I myself will
go. *[Demetrius exits]*

HELENA:
Oh, I am out of breath! But who is
here? Lysander! on the ground! Dead?
or asleep? Lysander, if you are alive,
good sir, awake.

LYSANDER: *[waking up quickly]*
And run through fire for your sweet
sake. Where is Demetrius? Oh, that name—
I could kill it with my sword!

HELENA:
Don't say that, Lysander; say that not.
Even if he does love your Hermia—lord,
so what? Hermia still loves you; so
be happy.

LYSANDER:
Happy with Hermia? No: I'm sorry for
all the time I have wasted on her. It's
not Hermia, but Helena that I love!

HELENA:
Was I born to be a laughing stock? What
did I do to deserve this? Truthfully,
this isn't right—in truth it's not—
for you to woo me like this is pure
rot. Oh, that a lady, refused by one
should then by another be treated like
scum! *[she exits]*

LYSANDER:
Hermia, stay sleeping; there while
Lysander gets himself out of here.
[Lysander exits]

HERMIA: *[waking with a start]*
Help me, Lysander! *[recovering a*

Act Two · Scene 2 **original abridged**	Act Two · Scene 2 **stage directions**

HELENA:
O, wilt thou leave me? Do not so.

DEMETRIUS:
Stay, on thy peril; I alone will go.
[Demetrius exits]

(exits UR)

HELENA:
O, I am out of breath! But who is
here? Lysander! on the ground! Dead?
or asleep? Lysander, if you live,
good sir, awake.

(sits on stool near Lys)

*(Lys snores and rolls over,
Hel notices him)*
(she shakes him)

LYSANDER: [waking up quickly]
And run through fire I will for thy
sweet sake. Where is Demetrius? Oh,
how fit a word is that vile name
to perish on my sword!

*(a changed Lys, under the
influence of the love-juice
he is more ardent and less
sensible, he kneels at Hel feet)*

HELENA:
Do not say so Lysander; say not
so. What though he love your Hermia?—
Lord, what though? Yet Hermia still
loves you; then be content.

(somewhat puzzled)

LYSANDER:
Content with Hermia? No: I do repent
the tedious minutes I with her have
spent. Not Hermia, but Helena I love!

*(even more ardently,
he buries his head on
her lap)*

HELENA:
Wherefore was I to this keen mockery
born? When at your hands did I deserve
this scorn? Good troth, you do me
wrong—good sooth you do—in such
disdainful manner me to woo. Oh, that
a lady, of one man refused, should
of another therefore be abused! [she
exits]

*(stands up in a huff,
thinking he's kidding)*

(she exits UR)

LYSANDER:
Hermia, sleep thou there; and never
come Lysander near!
[Lysander exits]

*(glancing at Her then
tiptoes off after Hel)*

HERMIA: [waking with a start]
Help me, Lysander! [recovering a

*(waking from a nightmare,
with a scream, she sits up)*

Act Two · Scene 2   vernacular

bit] Oh, dear me! What a dream I had!
Lysander, oh, it was really bad!
Lysander! Lysander! Oh no,
where are you? Say something
or I'll faint from fear. No? Then I
guess you're really not here. Either
my death or you I'll find out there.
[exits]

Act Three · Scene 1   scene description

The workmen now come on to this same spot to rehearse their play. (Titania is still sleeping.) Before they get to the actual rehearsal, they bring up various problems that they have discovered about the play and the acting of it.

With Bottom pretty much taking charge, they arrive at solutions for these problems and then they start the rehearsal.

Puck comes upon this scene and decides to make himself invisible and listen in. When Pyramus exits into the bushes, Puck takes the opportunity to follow him off and using his fairy magic, he fastens an asses head onto Bottom and then sits back and watches while "all hell breaks loose" when Bottom reenters and his pals see him.

They all run away from him in terror, and he, not aware that anything has happened to him, thinks that they are all just trying to frighten him and he decides to sing to prove that he is not afraid.

His singing wakes Titania and since Bottom is the first creature she sees, she falls in love with him. She then calls her fairies to wait upon him and escort him to her bower (the flowered, tree-shaded spot in the woods where she lives some of the time.) They all exit.

Act Three · Scene 1   vernacular

*[Titania is still asleep; enter Bottom,
Quince, Snout, Starveling, Snug and Flute]*
BOTTOM:
Are we all here?

QUINCE:
And on time. This is a marvelous spot
for our rehearsal.

BOTTOM:
Peter Quince—

QUINCE:
What is it Bottom?

BOTTOM:
There are things in this comedy of
Pyramus and Thisbe that will offend.
First, Pyramus has to draw a sword to
kill himself; which ladies couldn't
stand. What do you think?

STARVELING:
I think we must leave out the killing,
when all is done.

BOTTOM:
Not at all—I have a plan to solve
the problem. Write a little speech:
and let it say that we won't really
hurt anyone with our swords; and that
Pyramus is not dead—really. This will
keep them from being afraid.

QUINCE:
Well, we'll write it.

Act Two · Scene 2 **original abridged**

bit] Ay me, for pity! What a dream
was here! Lysander, look how I do
quake with fear! Lysander!
Lysander! Alack, where are
you? Speak, I swoon almost with
fear. No? Then I well perceive you
are not nigh. Either death, or you,
I'll find immediately.*[exits]*

Act Three · Scene 1 **original abridged**

*[Titania is still asleep; enter Bottom,
Quince, Snout, Starveling, Snug, and Flute]*

BOTTOM:
Are we all met?

QUINCE:
Pat. And here's a marvelous convenient
place for our rehearsal.

BOTTOM:
Peter Quince—

QUINCE:
What sayest thou Bottom?

BOTTOM:
There are things in this comedy of
Pyramus and Thisbe that will never
please. First, Pyramus must draw
a sword to kill himself; which the
ladies cannot abide. How answer you
that?

STARVELING:
I believe we must leave the killing
out, when all is done.

BOTTOM:
Not a whit—I have a device to make
all well. Write me a prologue: and
let the prologue say, we will do no
harm with our swords; and that Pyramus
is not killed—indeed. This will put
them out of fear.

QUINCE:
Well, we will have such a prologue.

Act Two · Scene 2   **stage directions**

(looks about for him)

(exits DR looking for Lys)

Act Three · Scene 1 **stage directions**

*(Q enters from UL, sits on DL stool with
his papers on his lap, B comes on from   UC,
crosses to R of Q, F and Sno from L,
sit R of Q, St and Snug enter from DL
and sit below Q)*

(indicating center stage)

(having the solution already)

SNOUT:
Won't the ladies be afraid of the
lion?

BOTTOM:
Men, bringing a lion into a room full
of ladies, is a dreadful thing.

SNOUT:
Then another speech should say that
he is not really a lion.

BOTTOM:
We'll have to state his name, and half
his face must show, and he must say:
"Ladies," or "Fair ladies, I wish you,"
or "I beg you not to be afraid. If you
think I'm really a lion, I'm not, I'm
a man."

QUINCE:
Well, we'll do it. But there are
two problems—one is, to get moonlight
inside a room: because you know,
Pyramus and Thisbe meet by moonlight.

SNOUT:
Does the moon shine the night we play
our play?

BOTTOM:
A calendar, a calendar! Look in the
almanac; find out moonshine, find
out moonshine.

QUINCE: *[looking it up]*
Yes, it does shine that night.

BOTTOM:
Why then, leave a window open,
and the moon may shine in.

QUINCE:
Yes, or else someone must come in
with a lantern and say he comes
to represent moonshine. Then there
is another thing: we must have a

SNOUT:
Will not the ladies be afeard of
the lion?

BOTTOM:
Masters, to bring in a lion among
ladies, is a most dreadful thing.

SNOUT:
Therefore, another prologue must tell
he is not a lion.

BOTTOM:
You must name his name, and half
his face must be seen, and he must
say, "Ladies," or "Fair ladies, I
would wish you," or "I would entreat
you, not to fear. If you think I am
a lion, I am no such thing, I am
a man."

QUINCE:
Well, it shall be so. But there is
two hard things—that is, to bring
the moonlight into a chamber: for
you know, Pyramus and Thisbe meet
by moonlight.

SNOUT:
Doth the moon shine that night we
play our play?

BOTTOM:
A calendar, a calendar! Look in the
almanac; find out moonshine, find
out moonshine.

QUINCE:
Yes, it doth shine that night.

BOTTOM:
Why then, leave a window open, and
the moon may shine in.

QUINCE:
Ay, or else one must come in with
a lantern and say he comes to present
the person of Moonshine. Then there
is another thing—we must have a

*(pulls out little book from his pocket,
all gather round to look at it)*

*(they all return to where
they were, relieved)*

wall; for Pyramus and Thisbe, the story says, talked through a crack in a wall.

SNOUT:
You could never bring in a wall. What do you say, Bottom?

BOTTOM:
Somebody must represent the Wall. And let him wear some plaster on him to signify a wall and let him hold his fingers like this, and through that crack Pyramus and Thisbe will whisper.

QUINCE:
Then all is well. Come, and rehearse your parts. Pyramus, you begin. When you have said your speech, enter into that thicket, and everybody else follow suit.

[Enter Puck, invisible to those onstage]
PUCK:
What a bunch of hicks are here so close to the Fairy Queen's bed? Is this a play? I'll listen.

QUINCE:
Speak, Pyramus.

BOTTOM: *[acting his part of Pyramus]*
"Thisbe, the flowers of odious savors sweet—"

QUINCE: *[correcting him]*
Odors, odors!

BOTTOM:
"Odors savors sweet. So hath thy breath, my dear. *[hears something]* But hark, a voice!" *[he exits to check out noise]*

PUCK: *[to audience]*
Weird! *[he follows Bottom off]*

FLUTE:
Do I speak now?

1. **Text**:

wall; for Pyramus and Thisbe, says
the story, did talk through the chink
of a wall.

SNOUT:
You can never bring in a wall. What
say you Bottom?

BOTTOM:
Some man must present Wall. And let
him have some plaster about him to
signify Wall and let him hold his
fingers thus, and through that cranny
shall Pyramus and Thisbe whisper.

QUINCE:
Then all is well. Come, and rehearse
your parts. Pyramus, you begin. When
you have spoken your speech, enter
into that brake; and so everyone
according to his cue.

[enter Puck, invisible to those
onstage]
PUCK:
What hempen homespuns have we here,
so near the cradle of the Fairy Queen?
What, a play? I'll be an auditor.

QUINCE:
Speak Pyramus.

BOTTOM: [acting his part of Pyramus]
"Thisbe, the flowers of odious savors
sweet—"

QUINCE: [correcting him]
Odors, odors!

BOTTOM:
"Odors savors sweet. So hath thy
breath, my dear. [hears something]
But hark, a voice!" [he exits]

PUCK: [to audience]
A strange Pyramus! [he follows Bottom
off]

FLUTE:
Must I speak now?

(demonstrates the 'cranny'
by making a circle with his
thumb and forefinger)

(Q shifts position so that
he's facing C, others sit
on ground behind him DL,
B goes to C, Q indicates
UL exit as the 'brake')

(enter P from UR, snaps
his fingers to become
invisible, crosses UC and
watches from there)

(directing from his stool)

(interrupting B)

(with his hand cupping his
ear, he pretends to hear
sound, exits UL)

(exits UL after B)

Act Three · Scene 1   vernacular

QUINCE:
Yes, you do, because he is going off
to see about a noise he heard and will
come back again.

FLUTE: *[as Thisbe]*
"Most radiant Pyramus, as true as truest
horse, that yet would never tire."

QUINCE:
Pyramus, enter. Your cue is past. It
is "never tire."

FLUTE: *[repeating the cue]*
"As true as truest horse, that yet would
never tire."

*[enter Puck invisible, and Bottom who
now wears asses-head]*
BOTTOM:
"If I were fair, fair Thisbe, I were
only thine."

QUINCE: *[reacting to the transformed
Bottom]*
Oh my god! We're haunted. Come on, guys,
let's go. Help! *[Quince, Flute, Snout,
Snug and Starveling exit]*

BOTTOM:
Why are they running away?

SNOUT: *[reentering]*
Oh Bottom, you've changed! *[he runs
off]*

QUINCE: *[reentering]*
Bottom, you've been transformed!
[exits]

BOTTOM:
I get it. They're trying to scare me.
But I won't budge from here. I'll walk
up and down, and I'll sing. Then they'll
hear I'm not afraid. *[he sings]*
    The ouzel cock, so black of hue,

QUINCE:
Ay, marry, must you. For he goes
but to see a noise that he heard
and is to come again.

FLUTE: *[as Thisbe]*
"Most radiant Pyramus, as true as
truest horse, that yet would never tire."

QUINCE:
Pyramus enter. Your cue is past;
it is "never tire."

FLUTE: *[repeating the cue]*
"As true as truest horse, that yet
would never tire."

*[enter Puck invisible, and Bottom
who now wears asses-head]*
BOTTOM:
"If I were fair, Thisbe, I were
only thine."

QUINCE: *[reacting to the transformed
Bottom]*
O monstrous! We are haunted. Pray
masters, fly! Help! *[Quince, Flute,
Snout, Snug and Starveling exit]*

BOTTOM:
Why do they run away?

SNOUT: *[reentering]*
O Bottom, thou art changed! *[he runs
off]*

QUINCE: *[reentering]*
Bottom, thou are translated!
[exits]

BOTTOM:
I see their knavery. This is to fright
me. But I will not stir from this
place. I will walk up and down here,
and I will sing. They shall hear
I am not afraid. *[he sings]*
    The ouzel cock, so black of hue,

(crosses C as Thisbe)

(calling UL)

*(B enters from UL crosses
to F)*
*(P enters and watches from
UL)*

*(exiting UL, L, DL, and
DR they scatter)*

(to audience)

*(runs on from where he
exited, sees B, runs off
another exit)*

*(runs on from where he
exited, runs off another
way)*

*(standing C amazed, comes
to this realization, then
walks from R to L across
stage)*

(make up whatever melody

With orange-tawny bill,

TITANIA: *[awakening]*
What angel awakens me from my slumber?

BOTTOM: *[still singing]*
  The throstle with his note
  so true,
  The wren with little quill.

TITANIA:
Kind mortal, my eyes are captivated
by you; and your sweetness drives me
to say—to swear—that I love you!

BOTTOM:
I think, lady, you don't have any reason
to say that. But, to tell the truth,
reason and love have little in common
these days.

TITANIA:
You are as clever as you are
beautiful.

BOTTOM:
If I had brains enough to get out of
these woods, that would be brains enough.

TITANIA:
Out of these woods! No! You shall stay
here whether you like it or not. I love
you. Therefore come with me. I'll give
you fairies to wait on you; *[calling]* Peaseblossom!
Cobweb! Moth! and Mustardseed! *[enter
four fairies]*

PEASEBLOSSOM:
Ready.

COBWEB:
And I.

MOTH:
And I.

Act Three · Scene 1 **original abridged**

With orange-tawny bill,

TITANIA: *[awakening]*
What angel wakes me from my flow'ry
bed?

BOTTOM: *[singing]*
The throstle, with his note so
true,
The wren with little quill.

TITANIA:
Gentle mortal, mine eye is enthralled
to thy shape; and thy virtue doth
move me to say—to swear—I love
thee!

BOTTOM:
Methinks, mistress, you should have
little reason for that. And yet,
to say truth, reason and love keep
little company together nowadays.

TITANIA:
Thou art as wise as thou art
beautiful.

BOTTOM:
If I had wit enough to get out of
this wood, I have enough.

TITANIA:
Out of this wood do not desire to
go; thou shalt remain here, whether
thou wilt or no. I do love thee.
Therefore go with me. I'll give thee
fairies to attend on thee; *[calling]*
Peaseblossom! Cobweb! Moth! and
Mustardseed! *[the four fairies enter]*

PEASEBLOSSOM:
Ready.

COBWEB:
And I.

MOTH:
And I.

Act Three · Scene 1 **stage directions**

*works for you, B is not a
great singer*)*

(sitting up on platform)

(crossing up to L of platform)

*(steps off platform and
crosses to L of B)*

*(enter from UR and jump
onto platform)*

Act Three · Scene 1   vernacular

MUSTARDSEED:
And I.

TITANIA:
Be kind and courteous to this gentleman.

PEASEBLOSSOM:
Hail, mortal!

COBWEB:
Hail!

MOTH:
Hail!

MUSTARDSEED:
Hail!

BOTTOM:
What is your name?

COBWEB:
Cobweb.

BOTTOM:
And your name, honest gentleman?

PEASEBLOSSOM:
Peaseblossom.

BOTTOM:
Your name, I beg you sir?

MUSTARDSEED:
Mustardseed.

TITANIA:
Come and wait on him; take him to my bower. *[they exit]*

Act Three · Scene 2   scene description

Oberon is wondering whether the love-juice has worked on Titania. Puck comes to tell him that Titania has awakened and that she has fallen in love with the actor playing Pyramus.

Oberon is delighted with the news. He then asks whether Puck has located the Athenian man. Puck says he has and just at that moment Demetrius

Act Three · Scene 2   vernacular

[enter Oberon]
OBERON:
I wonder if Titania has awakened. *[enter Puck]* Here comes my messenger. What's up, mad spirit?

Act Three · Scene 1 **original abridged**

MUSTARDSEED:
And I.

TITANIA:
Be kind and courteous to this
gentleman.

PEASEBLOSSOM:
Hail mortal!

COBWEB:
Hail!

MOTH:
Hail!

MUSTARDSEED:
Hail!

BOTTOM:
I beseech your name.

COBWEB:
Cobweb.

BOTTOM:
Your name, honest gentleman?

PEASEBLOSSOM:
Peaseblossom.

BOTTOM:
Your name, I beseech you sir?

MUSTARDSEED:
Mustardseed.

TITANIA:
Come, wait upon him; lead him to my
bower. *[they all exit]*

Act Three · Scene 2 **original abridged**

[enter Oberon]
OBERON:
I wonder if Titania be awaked. *[enter
Puck]* Here comes my messenger. How
now, mad spirit?

Act Three · Scene 1 **stage directions**

*(they each bow to B as
they speak)*

*(fairies exit UR with B and T following, P
trails behind stopping at UR exit)*

Act Three · Scene 2 **stage directions**

*(enters from L speaking,
sees P enter from UR, they
meet C)*

Act Three · Scene 2   scene description

Cont.

and Hermia enter. Oberon points out that Demetrius is the Athenian man he meant and Puck realizes that he anointed the wrong eyes.

Hermia (who obviously ran into Demetrius during her search for Lysander) is accusing Demetrius of killing Lysander because she can think of no other reason for Lysander to have left her alone in the woods.

Demetrius, of course denies this. Hermia leaves him to go on looking for Lysander. Demetrius realizes that there is no point in following her while she is so angry and decides to rest.

Oberon tells Puck to go and find Helena and to bring her back. He then squeezes the love-juice in Demetrius' eyes so that he will awaken when Helena arrives and fall in love with her.

Puck comes back and says that Helena and Lysander are about to enter and he and Oberon stand aside to watch.

Lysander is still pursuing Helena and she is still convinced that he is making fun of her. At that moment Demetrius awakens and he falls in love with Helena. Helena is now absolutely convinced that Demetrius and Lysander are in cahoots to torment her.

Then, on comes Hermia (who has been searching for Lysander all this time) and she races over to him and demands to know why he deserted her. Lysander tells her that he left because he hates her.

Hermia can't believe her ears and Helena, hearing all this now believes that Hermia is in on the joke with Lysander and Demetrius and that they are all trying to make fun of her. She is furious with Hermia and Hermia is furious with her because Hermia thinks that Helena has stolen her boyfriend.

At this point, the two guys start arguing about who loves Helena the most.

Helena says that she is going back to Athens but when she doesn't move, Hermia asks why she's not going and Helena says her heart won't let her leave. Hermia is afraid Helena means that she is in love with Lysander but Helena says no, it's Demetrius she loves.

The two guys now start arguing about who has the greater right to protect Helena against possible threats from Hermia and they go off to find a place to fight it out.

Left alone with Hermia and her spitfire temper, Helena decides to run away to avoid a fight.

Act Three · Scene 2   vernacular

PUCK:
My mistress is in love with a monster. Near to her bed, while she was still asleep, a bunch of crude workmen had come together to rehearse a play. Upon the dumbest of them, the one who played Pyramus, I attached an asses head. And at that moment it came to pass, Titania wakened and fell in love with an ass.

OBERON:
This has turned out better than I could have imagined. But did you pour the potion in the Athenian's eyes as I asked you to?

PUCK:
I did it while he was asleep. *[enter Demetrius and Hermia]*

OBERON:
This is that very Athenian.

PUCK:
This is the woman, but not the man. *[they stand aside]*

DEMETRIUS:
Oh, why do you scold me when I love you so?

HERMIA:
You have given me reason if you've killed Lysander. Would he have left me there asleep? It can only be that you have murdered him.

DEMETRIUS:
You stab me through the heart with your cruelty.

HERMIA:
You drive me past the limits of a young girl's patience. Have you killed him?

DEMETRIUS:
I am not guilty of shedding Lysander's blood, nor is he dead for all I know.

PUCK:
My mistress with a monster is in
love. While she was sleeping, a crew
of rude mechanicals were met together
to rehearse a play. The shallowest,
who Pyramus presented, an asses head
I fixed on him. And at that moment—
so it came to pass—Titania waked,
and straightway loved an ass.

(delighted with himself)

OBERON:
This falls out better than I could
devise. But hast thou yet latched
the Athenian's eyes with the love
juice, as I did bid thee do?

PUCK:
I took him sleeping. *[enter Demetrius
and Hermia]*

*(enter from DL, as soon as
they hit the stage, O and
P snap fingers to become
invisible*)*

OBERON:
This is the same Athenian.

PUCK:
This is the woman, but not the
man.*[Puck and Oberon stand aside]*

*(P and O sit on edge of
platform and watch)*

DEMETRIUS:
O, why rebuke you him that loves
you so?

*(Her sits on DL stool to rest for a
moment and Dem kneels L of her)*

HERMIA:
Thou hast given me cause to curse
if thou hast slain Lysander. Would
he have stolen away from sleeping
Hermia? It cannot be but thou hast
murdered him.

DEMETRIUS:
I'm pierced through the heart with
your stern cruelty.

HERMIA:
Thou driv'st me past the bounds of
maiden's patience. Hast thou slain
him?

*(stands angrily and crosses
C and turns back to him)*

DEMETRIUS:
I am not guilty of Lysander's blood; nor
is he dead for aught that I can tell.

*(he stands and crosses to
Her)*

Act Three · Scene 2 scene description	Act Three · Scene 2 vernacular

Cont.
Hermia, completely baffled by all that has happened, wanders off.

Oberon, who has been watching all this with Puck, now accuses him of negligence for placing the love-juice in the wrong man's eyes and Puck defends himself by pointing out that all Oberon had told him was to find the man wearing the Athenian garments and Lysander had on garments of Athens!

Oberon then devises a plan to remedy all the troubles. He needs to diffuse the fight and get Demetrius and Lysander to go to sleep so that he can counteract the love-juice in Lysander's eyes. In order to accomplish this, he tells Puck to pretend to be Demetrius and lead Lysander on a chase till he is worn out and then to pretend to be Lysander and lead Demetrius astray.

When they are both worn out and fall asleep, he tells Puck to apply the antidote herb into Lysander's eyes which will remove the effects of the love-juice and then Lysander will be back in love with Hermia. Oberon then leaves, telling Puck that he is going to ask Titania for the orphan boy and then release her from the spell.

Puck then proceeds to confuse and wear out Demetrius and Lysander as Oberon instructed him. And after Helena and Hermia both show up and fall asleep, Puck applies the antidote to Lysander's eyes.

HERMIA:
I beg you then, tell me that he is well.

DEMETRIUS:
And if I could, what do I get for my pains?

HERMIA:
The privilege of never seeing me again. *[she exits]*

DEMETRIUS:
It doesn't pay to follow when she's looking for a fight. So I'll just stay here for the rest of the night. *[he yawns and sleeps]*

OBERON:
What have you done? You've mistaken and put the love juice in some true-lover's eyes. Go through the woods and find Helena of Athens. Bring her here; I'll put the love juice in his eyes before she appears.

PUCK:
I go, I go, look how I go. *[he exits]*

OBERON: *[putting the juice in Demetrius' eyes]*
    When his love he does see,
    Let her shine as gloriously
    As does Venus up in the sky.
    When you wake, if she be by,
    Beg her for a good reply.

PUCK: *[reentering]*
Captain of our fairy band, Helena is here at hand, and the youth mistook by me. Lord, what fools these mortals be!

OBERON:
Stand aside. The noise they make will cause Demetrius to wake.
[they stand aside and Lysander and Helena enter]

HERMIA:
I pray thee, tell me then that he
is well.

DEMETRIUS:
And if I could, what should I get
therefore?

HERMIA:
A privilege never to see me more!
[she exits]

DEMETRIUS:
There is no following her in this
fierce vein. Here, therefore, for
a while I will remain. *[he yawns and
sleeps]*

OBERON:
What hast thou done? Thou hast
mistaken and laid the love juice
on some true-love's sight. About the
wood go, and Helena of Athens find.
Bring her here; I'll charm his eyes
for when she doth appear.

PUCK:
I go, I go; look how I go. *[he exits]*

OBERON: *[applying the nectar to
Demetrius' eye]*
    When his love he doth espy,
    Let her shine as gloriously
    As the Venus of the sky.
    When thou wak'st, if she be by,
    Beg of her for remedy.

PUCK: *[reentering]*
Captain of our fairy band, Helena
is here at hand; and the youth, mistook
by me. Lord, what fools these mortals
be!

OBERON:
Stand aside. The noise they make
will cause Demetrius to awake.
*[they stand aside and Lysander and
Helena enter]*

*(she pushes him away and exits
DR)*

*(he takes a step DR
looking off after Her,
yawns, lies down and
sleeps)*

*(O rises, crosses C looking
off DR and back to P)*

*(jumps up on platform,
runs off UR at warp speed)*
*(crosses to Dem, kneels,
squeezes love-juice into
into Dem eyes and chants)*

(enters UL crossing towards O)

*(O and P sit on edge of
platform and watch as Hel
strides DC from UL with Lys
following behind her)*

LYSANDER:
Why do you think I'd woo just to make
fun of you?

HELENA:
These vows belong to Hermia.

LYSANDER:
When I swore my love to her, I was so
callow.

HELENA:
And now, in dumping her, you prove you're
shallow.

DEMETRIUS: *[waking up]*
Oh Helen, goddess, nymph, my dove! What
shall I do to prove my love?

HELENA:
Oh spite! Oh hell! You are all making
fun of me; I can tell. If you were
men, as you appear to be, you wouldn't
be so cruel to me.

LYSANDER:
You are mean Demetrius; don't be
so; for you love Hermia: you know
I know.

HELENA:
You are all just wasting your
breath.

DEMETRIUS:
Lysander, you keep Hermia; if I ever
loved her, all that love is gone.
Look, here she comes; there is your
love.

HERMIA: *[entering]*
Why did you, so cruelly, leave
me?

LYSANDER:
Why should I stay, when love is forcing
me to go.

LYSANDER:
Why should you think that I should woo in scorn?

(speaking as he enters)

HELENA:
These vows are Hermia's.

(Hel stops C and turns to Lys)

LYSANDER:
I had no judgment when to her I swore.

(stops L of Hel)

HELENA:
Nor none in my mind, now you give her o'er.

(Hel crossing DR as if to exit, trips over Dem ending DR of him, Dem awakes, sees her and speaks)

DEMETRIUS: *[waking up]*
O Helen, goddess, nymph, divine!
To what, my love, shall I compare thine eyne?

HELENA:
O spite! O hell! I see you all are bent to set against me for your merriment. If you were men, as men you are in show, you would not use a gentle lady so.

LYSANDER:
You are unkind Demetrius; be not so; for you love Hermia: this you know I know.

(crossing to Dem)

HELENA:
Never did mockers waste more idle breath.

DEMETRIUS:
Lysander, keep thy Hermia; if e'er I loved her, all that love is gone. Look, where thy love comes; yonder is thy dear.

(Her is coming on from L)

HERMIA: *[entering]*
Why unkindly didst thou leave me so?

(crosses directly to Lys)

LYSANDER:
Why should he stay whom love doth press to go?

HERMIA:
What love could force Lysander away
from me?

LYSANDER:
Lysander's love—that would not let
him stay. Fair Helena; who more
brightly paints the sky at night
than all the stars with all their
light. Why do you seek me? You must
know, that hate I feel for you made
me go.

HERMIA:
You can't mean that; it can't be.

HELENA:
Oh, she is part of this confederacy!
Now I see, they have all joined
forces to make fun of me. Cruel
Hermia!—are you with them and
against me? Is all the time that
we have spent, our vows, our
schemes,—have you forgot?—our
schooldays' friendship, childhood
innocence? Will you tear our friendship apart to join with men and break
my heart? This isn't friendly; it
isn't maidenly.

HERMIA:
I am amazed at what you say. I'm not
making fun of you; you're making fun
of me!

HELENA:
Did you not get Lysander to follow
me and sing my praises? And made
your other love, Demetrius, call
me goddess? Why would he say that to
someone he hates?

HERMIA:
I don't understand what you mean!

Act Three · Scene 2 **original abridged**

Act Three · Scene 2 **stage directions**

HERMIA:
What love could press Lysander from
my side?

LYSANDER:
Lysander's love—that would not let
him bide. Fair Helena; who more
engilds the night than all yon fiery
oes and eyes of light. Why seeks't
thou me? Could not this make thee
know, the hate I bear thee made me
leave thee so?

*(indicating Hel, then turning
to Hel)*
(turning back to Her)

HERMIA:
You speak not as you think, it cannot
be.

HELENA:
Lo, she is one of this confederacy!
Now I perceive, they have joined all
three, to fashion this sport in spite
of me. Injurious Hermia!—have you
with these contrived to bait me?
Is all the counsel we have shared,
the vows, the hours that we have
spent,—is all forgot? all schooldays'
friendship, childhood innocence?
And will you rend our ancient love
asunder, to join with men in scorning
your poor friend? It is not friendly;
'tis not maidenly.

(turning out to audience)

*(crossing up between Lys
and Her)*

HERMIA:
I am amazed at your words. I scorn
you not; it seems that you scorn
me!

HELENA:
Have you not set Lysander to follow
me and praise my eyes and face? And
made your other love, Demetrius,
to call me goddess? Wherefore speaks
he this to her he hates?

HERMIA:
I understand not what you mean by
this!

HELENA:
If you had any manners, you wouldn't treat me like this. So, farewell.

LYSANDER:
Stay, gentle Helena, my love, my life, my soul, fair Helena!

HELENA:
Oh, great!

HERMIA: *[to Lysander]*
My dear, don't make fun of her.

LYSANDER:
Helen, I love you; on my life it's true.

DEMETRIUS:
I say I love you more than he can do.

LYSANDER: *[to Demetrius]*
If you say so, come on and prove it.

DEMETRIUS: *[to Lysander]*
Come on!

LYSANDER: *[to Hermia]*
Get off, vile thing! Let me go; or I will throw you off.

HERMIA:
Why are you so mean to me? What's caused this change my love?

LYSANDER:
Your love? Get lost, you worm! You witch, go away!

HERMIA:
Are you kidding?

HELENA:
He is, and so are you.

HELENA:
If you have any manners, you would
not make me such an argument. But,
fare you well.

(starts to cross DL)

LYSANDER:
Stay, gentle Helena, my love, my
life, my soul, fair Helena!

*(running and cutting her
off at the pass, he kneels
DL of Hel stopping her from
leaving, takes her left hand)*

HELENA:
O, excellent!

HERMIA: *[to Lysander]*
Sweet, do not scorn her so.

LYSANDER:
Helen, I love thee; by my life I
do.

DEMETRIUS:
I say I love thee more than he can do.

*(crossing to Hel, he kneels
R of Hel and grabs her right hand)*

LYSANDER: *[to Demetrius]*
If thou say so, withdraw, and prove
it too.

(still on his knees)

DEMETRIUS: *[to Lysander]*
Come!

*(starts off DR, Lys starts to follow,
Her crosses DR and grabs Lys arm,
he tries to shake loose of Her)*

LYSANDER: *[to Hermia]*
Off, vile thing! Let loose; or I
will shake thee from me.

HERMIA:
Why are you grown so rude? What change
is this sweet love?

(still holding him)

LYSANDER:
Thy love? Out, loathed med'cine!
O, hated potion, hence!

*(still trying to shake
her off)*

HERMIA:
Do you not jest?

HELENA:
Yes, and so do you.

Act Three · Scene 2   vernacular

LYSANDER:
Demetrius, I'll be right there.

DEMETRIUS: *[sarcastically]*
Sure you will.

LYSANDER:
What? Do you want me to hurt her? I
may hate her, but I will not harm her.

HERMIA:
Hate me! Oh my! Then you meant to leave
me in the woods alone?

LYSANDER:
Yes, and never wished to see you
again. For real, I hate you, and I
love Helena.

HERMIA:
Oh my! You cheater! you thief of love!
You snuck right in and stole my true
love's heart!

HELENA:
Yeah, yeah! you phony, you little
puppet!

HERMIA:
Puppet? Now I see, she has compared
our heights, and with her person,
her tall person, her height, for
god's sake, she has won him. And
have you grown so high in his esteem
because I am so dwarfish and so low?
How low am I? I'm not so low that
my nails can't reach into your eyes.

HELENA:
I beg you, gentleman, don't let her
hurt me. Maybe you think because she
is somewhat lower than me, that I can
fight her.

LYSANDER:
Demetrius, I will keep my word with
thee.

DEMETRIUS:
I'll not trust your word.

LYSANDER:
What, should I hurt her? Although
I hate her, I'll not harm her.

HERMIA:
Hate me! O me, what news! Why then
you left me—in earnest?

LYSANDER:
Ay, and never did desire to see thee
more. Be certain, I do hate thee,
and love Helena.

HERMIA:
O me! You juggler! you thief of love!
What, have you come by night, and stol'n
my love's heart?

*(lets go of Lys arm,
and crosses to Hel)*

HELENA:
Fie, fie! you counterfeit, you puppet,
you!

HERMIA:
Puppet! Now I perceive, she hath
made compare between our statures,
and with her personage, her tall
personage, her height, forsooth, she
hath prevailed with him. And are
you grown so high in his esteem
because I am so dwarfish and so low?
How low am I? Speak! I am not yet
so low but that my nails can reach
unto thine eyes.

*(crossing back to Lys
and Dem)*

(turning back to Hel)

*(goes for Hel and Lys
and Dem grab her by the
arms and hold her, Lys on
her left, Dem on right)*

HELENA:
I pray you, gentlemen, let her not
hurt me. You perhaps may think,
because she is something lower than
myself, that I can match her.

56   A Midsummer Night's Dream

Act Three · Scene 2   vernacular

HERMIA:
Lower! You hear that,—again!

HELENA:
Dear Hermia, don't be so nasty. I
always loved you, Hermia, always kept
your secrets—except that, because
I love Demetrius, I told him of your
plan to escape into the woods. I'm
going back to Athens and I won't follow
you anymore.

HERMIA:
Then go. Who's stopping you?

HELENA:
My foolish heart that wants to stay
here.

HERMIA:
Who with, Lysander?

HELENA:
With Demetrius.

LYSANDER: *[trying to protect Helena]*
Don't worry. She won't harm you
Helena.

HELENA:
Oh when she's angry, she is mean and
nasty. She was a vixen when she went
to school, and although she's little,
she is fierce.

HERMIA:
Little again? Why do you let her
pick on me like this? Let me at
her.

LYSANDER:
Get lost you dwarf; you minimus.

DEMETRIUS:
Don't say one word about Helena or
try to take up for her. If you even
think of loving her, you'll pay bigtime.

Act Three · Scene 2 **original abridged**

HERMIA:
Lower! Hark, again!

HELENA:
Good Hermia, do not be so bitter
with me. I evermore did love you,
Hermia, did ever keep your counsels,
save that in love unto Demetrius,
I told him of your stealth unto this
wood. To Athens will I go, and follow
you no further.

HERMIA:
Why, get you gone. Who is't that
hinders you?

HELENA:
A foolish heart that I leave here
behind.

HERMIA:
What, with Lysander?

HELENA:
With Demetrius.

LYSANDER: [trying to protect Helena]
Be not afraid, she shall not harm
thee Helena.

HELENA:
O when she is angry, she is keen
and shrewd. She was a vixen when
she went to school, and though she
be but little, she is fierce.

HERMIA:
Little again? Why will you suffer
her to flout me thus? Let me come
to her.

LYSANDER:
Get you gone you dwarf; you minimus.

DEMETRIUS:
Speak not of Helena; take not her
part. If thou dost intend love to
her, thou shalt aby it.

Act Three · Scene 2 **stage directions**

(struggling to break
loose)

(turns as if to exit DL
but doesn't move)

(still facing DL)

(turns back to them)

(struggling to get to her)

(Dem and Lys still holding
her back)

(saying this to Lys)

LYSANDER:
She's not holding me now; come on, follow me now, if you dare.

DEMETRIUS:
Follow? Heck, I'm with you, side by side. *[they exit]*

HERMIA:
You mistress, all this mess is due to you. Don't back away.

HELENA:
I don't trust you. Your hands are too quick to pick a fight. But I have longer legs to take flight. *[she exits]*

HERMIA:
I am dumbfounded by this sight. *[she exits]*

OBERON: *[to Puck]*
This is all your fault.

PUCK:
I made a mistake. Didn't you say I would know the man by his Athenian clothes?

OBERON:
These fellows are looking for a place to fight, go, Robin, blot out the moonlight; and lead these rivals all astray and keep them out of each other's way. Sometimes imitate Lysander's voice; then rant like Demetrius. Until, worn out with sleep, they drop off their feet. Then squeeze the juice of this herb into Lysander's eyes, it has the power to counteract the other charm. When they awake, all that has happened will seem a dream. I'm going to the Fairy Queen's to ask for the boy; and then I will release her from the charm and all will be at peace. *[he exits]*

Act Three · Scene 2 **original abridged**	Act Three · Scene 2 **stage directions**

LYSANDER:
Now she holds me not; now follow,
if thou dar'st.

(lets go of Her, crosses in front of Her to Dem, starts to exit DL below Hel)

DEMETRIUS:
Follow? Nay, I'll go with thee,
cheek by jowl. *[they exit]*

(Dem crosses to Lys and they exit together DL)

HERMIA:
You mistress, all this coil is long
of you. Nay, go not back.

(Her crosses to Hel, Hel retreats)

HELENA:
I will not trust you. Your hands
are quicker for a fray, my legs are
longer though, to run away. *[she
exits]*

(runs off L)

HERMIA:
I am amazed, and know not what to
say. *[she exits]*

(follows off L)

OBERON:
This is thy negligence.

(stands, crosses L to where they exited, turns back to P)
(crossing to O)

PUCK:
I mistook. Did not you tell me I
should know the man by the Athenian
garments he had on?

OBERON:
These lovers seek a place to fight,
hie Robin, overcast the night; and
lead these rivals so astray as one
come not within another's way. Like
to Lysander sometime frame thy tongue;
and sometime rail thou like Demetrius.
Till o'er their brows, sleep with
leaden legs doth creep. Then crush
this herb into Lysander's eye,
whose liquor hath this property, to take
all error from his sight. When they
next wake, all this derision shall
seem a dream. I'll to my Queen and
beg her Indian boy; and then I will
release her and all things shall
be peace. *[he exits]*

(takes other flower from his belt)

(exits UR)

PUCK:
Up and down, up and down, I will lead
them up and down. Here comes one.
[Lysander enters]

LYSANDER:
Where are you, Demetrius? Say something.

PUCK: *[imitating Demetrius]*
I'm here, villain. Where are you?

LYSANDER:
I'm coming.

PUCK: *[in Demetrius voice]*
Follow me then. *[exits]*

DEMETRIUS: *[enters]*
Lysander, you coward, did you run away?
Where are you hiding?

PUCK: *[imitating Lysander's voice]*
You coward! Come on! I'll whip you.

DEMETRIUS:
Yeah, where are you?

PUCK: *[imitating Lysander]*
Follow my voice. *[he runs off with
Demetrius following]*

LYSANDER: *[enters]*
He runs before me and dares me.
But when I get there, he is gone.
[he yawns] I'll rest here, *[he lies
down]* and wait for the daylight to
revenge this spite. *[he sleeps]*

Act Three · Scene 2 **original abridged**

Act Three · Scene 2 **stage directions**

(P indicates darkening the night by extending his arms overhead and bringing them down to his sides, saying "whoosh")
(doing a little dance)
(snaps his fingers for invisibility,* Lys enters from DL having trouble seeing in the dark)

PUCK:
Up and down, up and down, I will lead them up and down. Here comes one. *[enter Lysander]*

LYSANDER: *[enters]*
Where art thou Demetrius? Speak.

PUCK: *[imitating Demetrius' voice]*
Here villain. Where art thou?

(crossing DR around stool)

LYSANDER:
I will be with thee straight.

(trying to follow DR)

PUCK: *[in Demetrius' voice]*
Follow me then. *[exits]*

(exits UR with Lys following the voice)

DEMETRIUS:*[enters]*
Lysander, thou coward, art thou fled? Where dost thou hide?

(Dem enters DL to DL stool)

PUCK: *[imitating Lysander's voice]*
Thou coward! Come! I'll whip thee.

(enters from UR crosses to C)

DEMETRIUS:
Yea, art thou there?

(crosses to the voice, P ducks under his arms to UL)

PUCK: *[imitating Lysander's voice]*
Follow my voice. *[he exits with Demetrius following]*

(exits UL with Dem following)

LYSANDER: *[enters]*
He goes before me and dares me on. When I come where he calls, then he is gone. *[he yawns]* Here will I rest me. Come gentle day! Once thou show me thy light, I'll revenge this spite. *[he sleeps]*

(Lys enters UR, crosses DRC speaking as he moves)
(P enters from UL, meets Lys and "boings"* him to sleep when Lys says "gone")
(Lys sleeps DR, P exits UL)

PUCK: *[enter imitating Lysander's voice]*
Ho, ho, ho! Coward, where are you?

DEMETRIUS:
You run before me, all over the place; and don't dare stand still, and look me in the face. Where are you now?

PUCK:
Come on; I'm here.

DEMETRIUS:
No, you're just making fun of me. *[he yawns]* Go away. *[sleeps]*

HELENA: *[enters]*
Oh, what a night. A long and tedious night. *[she yawns]* Sleep, take me away. *[she sleeps]*

PUCK:
Only three? Come on, one more; two of both kinds adds up to four.

HERMIA: *[entering]*
I've never been so tired, never so depressed, I can't go another inch, *[she yawns]* so here, will I rest. *[she sleeps]*

PUCK: *[squeezing the herb into Lysander's eyes]*
    On the ground
    Sleep sound:
    I'll apply
    To your eye,
    Gentle lover, remedy.
    When thou wak'st,
    Thou tak'st
    True delight
    In the sight
    Of thy former lady's eye:
    Jack shall have Jill;
    Naught shall go ill;
The man shall have his mare again, and all shall be well.*[exit]*

Act Three • Scene 2 **original abridged**	Act Three • Scene 2 **stage directions**
PUCK: *[enter imitating Lysander's voice]* Ho, ho, ho! Coward, why com'st thou not?	*(runs on from UL and shifts back and forth in LC area with Dem having stopped at UL entrance looking back and forth trying to follow the voice)*
DEMETRIUS: Thou runn'st before me, shifting every place; and dar'st not stand, nor look me in the face. Where art thou now?	
PUCK: Come hither; I am here.	*(Puck crosses DL)*
DEMETRIUS: Nay then, thou mocks't me.*[yawns]* Go thy way.*[sleeps]*	*(crosses DL, searching, finds no one, P "boings"* him, he yawns, and sleeps L of stool)*
HELENA: *[entering]* O weary night, O long and tedious night. *[yawns]* Sleep, steal me awhile from mine own company. *[she sleeps]*	*(enters DL, crosses R two steps, says first line, P "boings" her, she yawns, lies down, sleeps DLC)*
PUCK: Yet but three? Come one more; two of both kinds makes up four.	*(crossing C and counting)*
HERMIA: *[entering]* Never so weary, never so in woe, I can no further crawl, no further go. *[yawns]* Here will I rest me. *[sleeps]*	*(enter SR, says her first line, P "boings" her, lies down sleeps where she is)*

PUCK: *[squeezing the juice into Lysander's eyes]*
  On the ground
  Sleep sound:
  I'll apply
  To your eye,
  Gentle lover, remedy.
  When thou wak'st,
  Thou tak'st
  True delight
  In the sight
  Of thy former lady's eye:
  Jack shall have Jill;
  Naught shall go ill;
The man shall have his mare again, and all shall be well.*[exit]*
	(crosses to Lys and squeezes the love-juice in his eyes, reciting)

	(exits DR)

Act Four · Scene 1 scene description	Act Four · Scene 1 vernacular

scene description

Titania and Bottom come onstage along with Titania's fairies. Oberon hides and watches them.

Titania is fawning over Bottom and her fairies are catering to his every whim. Bottom becomes sleepy and he and Titania take a nap.

At this point, Puck joins Oberon and Oberon tells him that he has gotten the boy from Titania and that he will now release her from the charm.

Titania awakens and wonders at what she calls the "visions" that she has seen. Oberon instructs Puck to remove the asses head from Bottom. And as the three of them depart, leaving Bottom asleep onstage, Titania asks for an explanation of what has happened.

At this point, Theseus, Hippolyta and Egeus enter and see the lovers asleep on the ground. Theseus assumes that they have gotten up early to celebrate May Day. He then remembers that this is also the day that Hermia is to make her choice. They awaken the young lovers.

Theseus then asks the boys how come they are sleeping together so peacefully when he knows them to be enemies.

Lysander, still in a daze, says that he came to the forest with Hermia intending to escape the laws of Athens. Upon hearing this, Egeus starts screaming for justice. But when Demetrius explains that his love for Hermia is gone, Theseus decides to overrule the law of Athens. He announces that the couples: Lysander and Hermia, and Demetrius and Helena, will be married along with Hippolyta and himself. They all exit.

Bottom, who has been asleep all this time, awakens and is obviously disoriented. He thinks that he has had a bizarre dream and that he should get Quince to write a poem about it. He then exits.

vernacular

[the four lovers are asleep onstage, Titania, Bottom, and the fairies enter —Oberon enters behind them, unseen by them]

TITANIA: *[to Bottom]*
Come, sit down upon this flowerbed, while I stick roses in your sleek smooth head.

BOTTOM:
Where's Peaseblossom?

PEASEBLOSSOM:
Here.

BOTTOM:
Scratch my head, Peaseblossom. Where's Monsieur Cobweb?

COBWEB:
Here.

BOTTOM:
Monsieur Cobweb, get your weapons and kill me a bee and bring me the honey. Where's Monsieur Mustardseed?

MUSTARDSEED:
Here. What do you wish?

BOTTOM:
Nothing, good Monsieur, except to help Cobweb to scratch. I must go to the barber's, I feel very hairy. *[he yawns]* I'm reclined to take a little nap.

TITANIA:
You sleep. Fairies, go.
Oh, how I love you! *[they both sleep]*

[enter Puck]
OBERON:
Welcome, good Robin. Do you see this

Act Four · Scene 1 **original abridged**	Act Four · Scene 1 **stage directions**
[the four lovers are asleep onstage, Titania, Bottom, and the fairies enter–Oberon enters behind them, unseen to them] TITANIA: *[to Bottom]* Come, sit thee down upon this flow'ry bed, while I stick roses in thy sleek smooth head.	*(T, B and fairies enter UR, O enters UL and stands in UL corner watching)* *(T leads B to DS side of platform, they sit, fairies kneel around them on floor, T puts roses in B head)*
BOTTOM: Where's Peaseblossom?	
PEASEBLOSSOM: Ready.	*(pops up)*
BOTTOM: Scratch my head, Peaseblossom. Where's Monsieur Cobweb?	*(Peaseblossom gets up on platform behind B and scratches him)*
COBWEB: Ready.	*(pops up)*
BOTTOM: Monsieur Cobweb, get you your weapons and kill me a bee and bring me the honey. Where's Monsieur Mustardseed?	*(Cobweb exits UR)*
MUSTARDSEED: Ready. What's your will?	*(pops up and bows)*
BOTTOM: Nothing, good Monsieur, but to help Cobweb to scratch. I must to the barber's, for methinks I am marvelous hairy about the face. *[he yawns]* I have an exposition of sleep come upon me.	*(gets up on platform and scratches B)*
TITANIA: Sleep thou. Fairies begone. O, how I love thee! *[they both sleep]*	*(she lies down next to him on the platform and holds him in her arms, B US of T, their heads are SR)*
[enter Puck] OBERON: Welcome, good Robin. Seest thou this	*(P enters in UL corner)*

sight? I begin to feel sorry for her.
When I met her recently near the woods,
I asked her for the orphan boy and right
away she gave me him. Now that I have
the boy, I will release the Fairy Queen.
[he applies the herb to her eyes]
   Be as thou wast wont to be,
   See as thou wast wont to see.
Now, my Titania, awaken, my sweet queen.

TITANIA: *[awakening]*
My Oberon! what strange visions I have
seen! I thought I was in love with an
ass.

OBERON:
There is your love.

TITANIA:
How did this come to pass?

OBERON:
Shhh! Robin, take off this head.

OBERON: *[continuing]*
Come, my queen, take hands with me.
We shall live together peacefully.

TITANIA:
My lord, as we go, tell me why I was
sleeping found, with these mortals on
the ground. *[all three exit]*

*[the sound of a hunting horn is heard
and Theseus, Hippolyta and Egeus
enter]*
THESEUS:
Let us go, fair queen, to the mountain
top. But hush! what nymphs are these?

EGEUS:
My lord, this is my daughter, and this,
Lysander, this is Demetrius, and this,
Helena. I wonder at their being here
together.

sight? Her dotage now I do begin
to pity. For meeting her of late
behind the wood, I did ask of her
her changeling child, which straight
she gave me. And now I have the boy,
I will release the Fairy Queen.
[he applies the nectar to her eyes]
  Be as thou wast wont to be,
  See as thou wast wont to see.
Now, my Titania, wake you, my sweet queen.

*(O crosses to T, squeezes
love-juice and recites)*

TITANIA: *[waking]*
My Oberon! what visions have I seen!
Methought I was enamored of an ass.

*(rolls DS, sees O and
sits up)*

OBERON:
There lies your love.

(pointing to sleeping B)

TITANIA:
How came these things to pass?

OBERON:
Silence awhile. Robin, take off this
head.

*(P crosses to B and removes
head and places it under
platform)*

OBERON: *[continuing]*
Come, my queen, take hands with me.
Now thou and I are new in amity.

*(they stand, take hands and
circling each other dance
off DL during the course
of their next lines, as
simply or elaborately as
the actors like, the point being,
they are engrossed in each other's
eyes, P follows them off happily)*

TITANIA:
My lord, in our flight, tell me how
it came that I sleeping here was
found, with these mortals on the
ground. *[all three exit]*

*[the sound of a hunting horn is heard
and Theseus, Hippolyta, and Egeus
enter]*
THESEUS:
We will, fair queen, up to the
mountain's top. But soft!
what nymphs are these?

*(offstage "actor" sound
effect,* enter UL, E R of
Th, Hip L of Th, they are
heading DR)*

(stops when he sees them)

EGEUS:
My Lord, this is my daughter here
asleep, and this Lysander, this
Demetrius is, this Helena. I wonder
of their being here together.

(indicating them)

THESEUS:
No doubt they got up early, and came here to bless our wedding day. But, Egeus, isn't this the day that Hermia must make her choice?

EGEUS:
It is, my lord.

THESEUS:
Wake them.

THESEUS: *[continuing]*
Good morning, friends.

LYSANDER:
My lord.

THESEUS:
I beg you all, stand up.
I know you two are rivals. What brought about this peace?

LYSANDER: *[still half asleep—in a daze]*
My lord. I truly cannot say. But, I think I came here with Hermia. We'd planned to escape from Athens.

EGEUS: *[furious]*
Enough, that's enough, my lord; the law, the law on his head. They were planning to run away.

DEMETRIUS:
My lord, fair Helen told me of their plan; and I, in a fury, followed them, Helena, in love, followed me. But, my lord, I don't know by what power—but by some power—my love to Hermia, melted like the snow. And now, with all my heart and soul, I love Helena. I was engaged to her, my lord, before I saw Hermia. But it was as though I were sick and couldn't want her love. But, now I am restored to health and

Act Four · Scene 1 **original abridged**	Act Four · Scene 1 **stage directions**

THESEUS:
No doubt they rose up early, and came
here in grace of our solemnity. But,
Egeus, is not this the day that Hermia
should give answer of her choice?

EGEUS:
It is, my Lord.

THESEUS:
Wake them.   *(they all "ahem" loudly)*

THESEUS: *[continuing]*   *(they begin to stir)*
Good morrow, friends.

LYSANDER:
My lord.

THESEUS:
I pray you all, stand up.   *(they stand)*
I know you two are rival enemies.   *(referring to Dem and Lys)*
How comes this gentle concord in
the world?

LYSANDER: *[still half asleep—in
a daze]*
My Lord, I cannot truly say. But,
I think I came with Hermia hither.
Our intent was to be gone from Athens.

EGEUS: *[furious]*
Enough, enough, my Lord; I beg the
law, the law, upon his head. They
would have stol'n away.

DEMETRIUS:
My Lord, fair Helen told me of their
purpose, and I in fury followed them,
Helena, in fancy, following me. But,
my Lord, I wot not by what power,
—but by some power it is—my love to
Hermia melted as the snow. And now
the object and the pleasure of mine   *(turning to Hel and
eye, is only Helena. To her, my Lord,   looking at her for the
was I betrothed ere I saw Hermia. But,   rest of the speech)*
like a sickness, did I loathe this
food. But, as in health, come to
my natural taste, now I do wish it,

I do wish her, love her, long for her,
and will forevermore be true to her.

THESEUS:
Fair lovers, we will talk more about
this later. Egeus, I will overrule the
law; and in the temple, in a little
while, along with us, these couples
shall be married. Let us all go to
Athens. Come, Hippolyta. *[they exit]*

DEMETRIUS:
All this seems small and indistinct,
like distant mountains turing into
clouds.

HERMIA:
I seem to see these things with
blurred vision when everything
appears double.

HELENA:
Me too. And I have found Demetrius
like a jewel, mine; but not really
mine.

DEMETRIUS:
Are you sure we're really awake? It
seems to me we're still dreaming.
Wasn't the Duke here and didn't he tell
us to follow him?

HERMIA:
Yes.

LYSANDER:
And he told us to follow him to the
temple.

DEMETRIUS:
Why then, we are awake. Let's follow
and as we go, let's recount our
dreams. *[they exit]*

BOTTOM: *[awakening but still half-asleep]*
When my cue comes, call me. *[waking
more]* Oh my God! I have had a
rare vision. I have had a dream.
I thought I was...I thought I

love it, long for it, and will
for evermore be true to it.

THESEUS:
Fair lovers, of this discourse we
more will hear anon. Egeus, I will
overbear your will; in the temple,
by and by with us, these couples
shall be knit. Away, with us, to Athens.
Come, Hippolyta. *[they exit]*

DEMETRIUS:
These things seem small and
undistinguishable, like far-off
mountains turned into clouds.

HERMIA:
Methinks I see these things with
parted eye, when everything seems
double.

HELENA:
So methinks. And I have found
Demetrius like a jewel, mine own,
and not mine own.

DEMETRIUS:
Are you sure that we are awake? It
seems to me that yet we sleep. Do
not you think, the Duke was here and
bid us follow him?

HERMIA:
Yea.

LYSANDER:
And he did bid us follow to the
temple.

DEMETRIUS:
Why then, we are awake. Let's follow,
and by the way, let us recount our
dreams. *[they exit]*

BOTTOM: *[waking but still in a daze]*
When my cue comes, call me. *[waking
more]* God's my life! I have had a
most rare vision. I have had a dream.
Methought I was—methought I

(Th, Hip and E exit UL)
*(during the following lines,
the lovers slowly cross
DSC and stand in a line
looking over the heads of
the audience, at the distant
mountains, they speak softly)*

(she looks at Dem)

*(he smiles at her and
takes Hel hand)*

(they slowly cross UL, exit)

*(sits up on edge of plat-
form, yawning and stretching)*
*(realizing where he is, he
slowly stands and crosses
DSC as he speaks)*

had...man's eye has not heard,
man's ear has not seen, man's
hand is not able to taste, his
tongue to conceive, nor his heart
to report what my dream was. I will
get Peter Quince to write a poem
about my dream. It will be called
"Bottom's Dream" because it has no
bottom! *[he exits]*

Act Four • Scene 2   **scene description**

In this scene we find Quince, Flute, Snout and
Starveling concerned about the whereabouts of
Bottom. Snug comes on with the news that the
Duke and Hippolyta along with the other couples,
are married

Just then Bottom comes running on and tells
them that their play is on the *short list* for the
Duke's entertainment and that everyone should get
ready and meet at the palace.

Act Four • Scene 2   **vernacular**

*[enter Quince, Flute, Snout and
Starveling]*
QUINCE:
Have you checked at Bottom's house?
Has he come home yet?

STARVELING:
Hasn't been heard of.

FLUTE:
If he doesn't show up, our play is
ruined.

SNUG: *[entering]*
Masters, the Duke is coming from the
temple, and there were two or three
other lords and ladies also married.

BOTTOM: *[entering excited]*
Where are you lads?

QUINCE:
Bottom! Oh, thank god!

BOTTOM:
Masters, the Duke has dined. Get your
costumes together; meet at once at the
palace; everybody, look over your parts;
for, the short and the long of it is,
our play has been picked. No more words;
Away! *[they all exit]*

Act Four · Scene 1 **original abridged**

had...The eye of man hath not heard, the ear of man hath not seen, man's hand is not able to taste, his tongue to conceive, nor his heart to report what my dream was. I will get Peter Quince to write a ballad of this dream. It shall be called "Bottom's Dream," because it hath no bottom! *[he exits]*

Act Four · Scene 1 **stage directions**

(crosses slowly UL and exits)

Act Four · Scene 2 **original abridged**

[enter Quince, Flute, Snout and Starveling]
QUINCE:
Have you sent to Bottom's house? Is he come home yet?

STARVELING:
Not heard of.

FLUTE:
If he come not, then the play is marred.

SNUG: *[entering]*
Masters, the Duke is coming from the temple, and there is two or three lords and ladies more, married.

BOTTOM: *[entering excited]*
Where are these lads?

QUINCE:
Bottom! O most happy hour!

BOTTOM:
Masters, the Duke hath dined. Get your apparel together; meet presently at the palace; every man look o'er his part; for, the short and the long is, our play is preferred. No more words; away! *[they all exit]*

Act Four · Scene 2 **stage directions**

(Q enters UC, F and Sno enter from L, St comes on DR, they all meet C)

(enters UR, crosses to others)

(comes on from UL, speaking as he enters)

(crosses to center of group)

(exit variously DL, DR and R)

Act Five · Scene 1   scene description

This scene takes place in the palace of the Duke. Theseus, Hippolyta, the lovers and Philostrate are gathered after dinner. Theseus asks Philostrate if there is a play to help wear away the evening between the wedding supper they have just finished and bedtime.

Philostrate says that while there is a play, it is not very good. Theseus wants to see it anyway and sends Philostrate to get the *actors.*

The actors enter and Quince proceeds to read the introductory speech that they have written which sums up the story of the play they are about to perform.

Snout comes forward and reads his speech which explains that he is portraying the wall that separates the two lovers, Pyramus and Thisbe.

Pyramus then comes on to his side of the wall and asks the wall to show the hole through which he might look to see Thisbe, which wall does. Pyramus looks through the hole and announces that he sees nothing.

Thisbe enters and chats with the wall. Pyramus hears her voice and asks her to meet him at Ninny's tomb. Thisbe agrees and they exit. Wall then exits.

Snug and Starveling come on representing Lion and Moonshine and both explain to the audience who they are. Then on comes Thisbe who lets the audience know that the setting is now "old Ninny's tomb."

Lion roars and scares Thisbe who drops her cloak and runs off. Lion then chews on the cloak leaving bloodstains on it—no doubt from previous kills—and he exits. Then Pyramus enters and when he sees the cloak stained with the blood, Pyramus assumes Thisbe has been killed and he proceeds to kill himself.

Thisbe then enters and sees that Pyramus is dead and she too commits suicide.

The actors all bow and the audience applauds and Bottom asks the Duke if he would like to see an encore piece. The Duke says no and the actors leave. Theseus announces that it is bedtime and all depart.

The fairies come on and at Oberon and Titania's command they bless the marriages and then depart leaving Puck alone onstage to bid farewell to the real audience.

Act Five · Scene 1   vernacular

[enter Hippolyta and Theseus]
HIPPOLYTA:
It's odd, Theseus, what these lovers speak of.

THESEUS:
More odd than true. I can never believe these fantastical stories, or these fairytales. Lovers and madmen both have such seething brains, such bizarre fantasies, that they conceive more than cool reason can ever dream of.

[the lovers and Philostrate enter]
THESEUS:
Joy, dear friends! joy and fresh days of love live in your hearts!
[to Philostrate] What shall we do to wear away the time between supper and bedtime What entertainment is there? Is there a play?

PHILOSTRATE:
There is, my lord, one that is brief, but dull: none of it makes any sense and the actors are dreadful.

THESEUS:
Who are the actors?

PHILOSTRATE:
Hard-working men from Athens who never used their brains till now.

THESEUS:
We'll hear it.

PHILOSTRATE:
No, my noble lord, you won't like it. I've heard it, and there's nothing to it; unless you'd enjoy making fun of them.

THESEUS:
I will hear that play; for nothing can be wrong when it is offered with sincerity and duty. Go, bring them in.

Act Five · Scene 1 **original abridged**

[enter Hippolyta and Theseus]
HIPPOLYTA:
'Tis strange, my Theseus, that these lovers speak of.

THESEUS:
More strange than true. I never may believe these antic fables, nor these fairy toys. Lovers and madmen have such seething brains, such shaping fantasies, that apprehend more than cool reason ever comprehends.

[the lovers and Philostrate enter]
THESEUS:
Joy, gentle friends! joy and fresh days of love accompany your hearts! *[to Philostrate]* What shall we have to wear away this long three hours between supper and bedtime? What revels are in hand? Is there no play?

PHILOSTRATE:
A play there is, my Lord, which is brief but tedious: there is not one word apt, one player fitted.

THESEUS:
What are they that do play it?

PHILOSTRATE:
Hard-handed men, that work in Athens, which never labored in their minds till now.

THESEUS:
We will hear it.

PHILOSTRATE:
No, my noble Lord, it is not for you. I have heard it, and it is nothing; unless you can find sport in their intents.

THESEUS:
I will hear that play; for never anything can be amiss, when simpleness and duty tender it. Go, bring them in.

Act Five · Scene 1 **stage directions**

(enter UL and cross to DR as they speak, Hip sits on DR stool, Th stands L of her)

(Phil leads them on from UL, Phil crosses DC, lovers are L of Phil)

(Phil goes off UR, leads them on, indicates C stage and platform for their use, they lay out the props and take various positions behind platform, the lovers sit in DL corner, TH moves to R

PHILOSTRATE:
With your Grace's permission, the
Prologue.

QUINCE: *[as the prologue, he reads
from his script]*
Gentles, this man is Pyramus, This
beautiful lady, Thisbe. This man,
with the lime and plaster, represents
Wall, that vile wall which kept these lovers
apart: and through the crack in
the wall, they whispered. This man
represents Moonshine: since by
moonshine they did meet at Ninus'
tomb, in order to woo. This grisly beast,
[Lion roars gently] Lion is his name, scared
away Thisbe, who had arrived first,
but as she fled, her cloak fell down,
and Lion, stained it with his bloody mouth.
Later, Pyramus comes and finds his trusty
Thisbe's cloak chewed up. He then, bravely
brings out his blade and bloodies his own
breast. Then Thisbe draws his dagger
and dies. Lion, Moonshine, Wall and
the lovers will fill in the rest of the
story. *[all exit except Wall]*

SNOUT: *[as Wall, reading from his
written speech]*
In this little play, it befalls, that
I, Snout's my name, must play a wall;
and such a wall as I would have you
think, that had in it a cranny, hole,
or chink, through which the lovers,
Pyramus and Thisbe, did often whisper,
very secretly.

BOTTOM: *[as Pyramus]*
Oh night, with sky so black—alack,
alack, alack! I fear my Thisbe's
promise is forgot! Oh wall, Oh lovely

Act Five · Scene 1 original abridged

PHILOSTRATE:
So please your Grace, the Prologue.

QUINCE: *[acting as the prologue, he reads from script]*
Gentles, this man is Pyramus,
this beauteous lady, Thisbe.
This man, with lime and roughcast,
doth present Wall, that vile Wall which
did these lovers sunder: and through
Wall's chink, they whisper. This man presenteth
Moonshine: for by moonshine did these
lovers meet at Ninus' tomb, there
to woo. This grisly beast, *[Lion roars gently]* Lion, by name,
Thisbe, coming first did
scare away: and, as she fled her
mantle did fall; which Lion,
with bloody mouth, did stain.
Anon comes Pyramus, and finds
his trusty Thisbe's mantle slain.
Whereat with blade, he bravely
broached his boiling bloody breast.
And Thisbe, his dagger drew, and
died. For all the rest, let Lion,
Moonshine, Wall and lovers twain,
at large discourse. *[players all exit except for Wall]*

SNOUT: *[as Wall, reading from his written speech]*
In this same interlude, it doth befall,
that I, one Snout by name, present
a wall: and such a wall as I would
have you think, that had in it a
crannied hole or chink, through which
the lovers, Pyramus and Thisbe, did
whisper often, very secretly.

BOTTOM: *[as Pyramus]*
Oh night, with hue so black—alack,
alack, alack! I fear my Thisbe's
promise is forgot! O wall, O lovely

Act Five · Scene 1 stage directions

of Hip, they all watch)
(Phil then crosses to DR corner, stands)
(Q comes to DR corner of platform)
(they each step forward and bow when they are introduced)

(wall demonstrates this, Pyramus and Thisbe pretend to whisper through chink)

(when Lion steps forward to bow, he roars gently)

(the actors mime this C stage, quickly and simply as Q describes these actions)

(they exit to behind the platform, wall stays C, Q stays in place with script to cue if needed)

(B crosses to L of wall)

wall, that stands between her
father's ground and mine, Oh wall,
Oh lovely wall, show me your chink
to blink through with my eye. *[wall shows
chink]* Thanks, courteous wall.
But what do I see? No Thisbe do I see.
[Flute enters]

FLUTE: *[as Thisbe]*
Oh wall, often have you heard my
moans for parting my fair Pyramus
and me.

BOTTOM: *[perks up at the sound of
Thisbe's voice]*
I see a voice! I will go to the
chink to spy if I can hear my Thisbe's
face. Thisbe!

FLUTE:
My love!

BOTTOM:
Oh, kiss me through the hole of this
vile wall.

FLUTE:
I kissed the wall's hole, not your
lips at all.

BOTTOM:
Will you meet me at Ninny's tomb right
away?

FLUTE:
I'll come without delay. *[they both
exit]*

SNOUT:
Now I, Wall, have done my part; and
so, being done, now I Wall, will go.
[he exits]

THESEUS:
Here come two noble beasts, a man
and a lion. *[Lion and Moonshine enter]*

Act Five · Scene 1 **original abridged**	Act Five · Scene 1 **stage directions**

wall, that stand'st between her
father's ground and mine, O wall,
O lovely wall, show me thy chink, to
blink through with mine eyne. *[wall
shows chink]* Thanks, courteous wall.
But what see I? No Thisbe do I see.
[Flute enters]

*(makes a circle with his
thumb and forefinger)*
*(B looks through chink
then out to "audience")*

FLUTE: *[as Thisbe]*
O wall, full often hast thou heard
my moans, for parting my fair Pyramus
and me.

*(speaking in a high-pitched,
"lady" voice)*

BOTTOM: *[perks up at the sound of
Thisbe's voice]*
I see a voice! Now will I to the
chink to spy an I can hear my Thisbe's
face. Thisbe!

(speaking through the chink)

FLUTE:
My love!

(speaking through chink)

BOTTOM:
O, kiss me through the hole of this
vile wall.

FLUTE:
I kiss the wall's hole, not your
lips at all.

*(trying to kiss through
chink)*
*(wall wipes 'kiss' off his
hand while F and B wipe
their lips)*

BOTTOM:
Wilt thou at Ninny's tomb meet me
straightway?

FLUTE:
I come without delay. *[they both
exit]*

*(they both cross to behind
platform)*

SNOUT:
Thus have I, Wall, my part discharged
so; and, being done, thus Wall away
doth go. *[he exits]*

(speaking to "audience")

(crosses US of platform)

THESEUS:
Here come two noble beasts in, a
man and a lion. *[Lion and Moonshine
enter]*

*(Snug and St come to C,
St has lantern, Snug is
wearing lion's head)*

SNUG: *[as Lion, reads his speech]*
You ladies, who fear the smallest
mouse that creeps on floors, may now
quake and tremble, when the rough lion
roars. But know that I am Snug, the
furniture-maker; and that I would
never come in strife—if I did, it
would probably cost me my life.

THESEUS:
A very gentle beast, and with a
good conscience. Let us hear the
moon.

STARVELING: *[as Moonshine]*
All that I have to say, is to tell
you, that the lantern is the moon
and I am the man in the moon.

DEMETRIUS:
Here comes Thisbe. *[Flute enters]*

FLUTE:
This is old Ninny's tomb. Where is my
love?

SNUG:
Oh! *[Lion roars and Thisbe exits]*

DEMETRIUS:
Excellent roaring, lion.

HIPPOLYTA:
Excellent shining, moon.

BOTTOM: *[entering]*
Sweet moon, I thank you for shining
so bright; for by your gracious
gleams I trust to take a taste of
Thisbe's sight. But wait! What sorry
sight is this! Your cloak and hood—
what, stained with blood? Oh, Nature,
why did you make lions, since it is
a vile lion that has

SNUG: *[as Lion]*
You ladies, who do fear the smallest
mouse that creeps on floor, may now
quake and tremble here, when lion
rough doth roar. But know that I,
Snug the joiner, am; for if I should
as lion come in strife into this
place, 'twere pity on my life.

THESEUS:
A very gentle beast, and of a good
conscience. Let us listen to the
Moon.

STARVELING: *[as Moonshine]*
All that I have to say, is to tell
you, that the lantern is the moon
and I am the man in the moon.

DEMETRIUS:
Here comes Thisbe. *[Flute enters]*

FLUTE:
This is old Ninny's tomb. Where is
my love?

SNUG:
O! *[Lion roars and Thisbe exits]*

DEMETRIUS:
Well roared, Lion.

HIPPOLYTA:
Well shone, Moon.

BOTTOM: *[enters]*
Sweet Moon, I thank thee for shining
now so bright; for, by thy gracious
gleams I trust to taste of Thisbe's
sight. But stay! What dreadful
dole is here! Thy mantle good,
what, stained with blood? O,
wherefore, Nature, didst thou lions
frame? Since lion vile hath here

*(speaking very gently so
no one will be afraid)*

*(Snug gets up on platform
and crouches as lion)*

(holding his lantern up)

*(gets up on platform and
holds lantern high)*

*(F has to repeat this line
twice because Snug misses
cue, Q is also trying to
cue Snug)*
*(realizing it's his cue,
he jumps off platform and
roars, F screams, drops
shawl and exits to behind
platform)*

*(Snug chews shawl leaving 'blood stained'
side of shawl up and exits to behind
platform)*

*(crosses to C wearing sword,
speaks up to St)*

(sees shawl, picks it up)

deflowered my dear: who is—
no, no—who was the fairest dame that
lived. Out, sword, and wound the breast
of Pyramus: yes, that left breast where
the heart does hop. Thus die I, thus, thus,
thus. Now I am dead, now I am fled, my
soul is in the sky. Tongue, lose your light!
Moon, take flight! *[the moon exits]*
Now die, die, die, die, die.

FLUTE: *[entering]*
Asleep, my love? *[realizing he is dead]*
What, dead, my dove? Oh Pyramus, arise!
Speak, speak. Quite dumb? Dead? Dead?
Tongue, not a word? Come, trusty sword;
come, blade, my breast cut through! Adieu,
adieu, adieu. *[Thisbe dies]*

BOTTOM:
Would you like to see the
epilogue?

THESEUS:
No epilogue, I beg you; your play needs
no explanation. For when all the players
are dead, what more need be said? *[players exit]*
Lovers, it's time for bed: it's almost fairy
time. *[they exit and the fairies enter]*

TITANIA:
Hand in hand, with fairy grace, we
will dance and bless this place.

OBERON:
    So shall all the couples three
    Ever true in loving be;
    Go away; do not stay;
    But meet again by break of day.
[they exit]

deflowered my dear: which is—no,
no—which was the fairest dame, that
lived. Out, sword, and wound the
pap of Pyramus: ay, that left pap,
where heart doth hop. Thus die I, thus,
thus, thus. Now am I dead, now am I
fled, my soul is in the sky. Tongue,
lose they light! Moon, take thy flight!
[the moon exits] Now die, die, die die,
die, die.

(pulls sword from his belt)

*(B stabs himself after each
'thus', falls to the ground, as
though dead, then remembers to
finish his speech)*
(St goes behind platform)
(B "dies" lying on his back)

FLUTE: *[entering]*
Asleep, my love? *[realizing he is
dead]* What, dead, my dove? O Pyramus,
arise! Speak, speak. Quite dumb?
Dead? Dead? Tongue, not a word! Come,
trusty sword; come, blade, my breast
imbrue! Adieu, adieu, adieu. *[Thisbe dies]*

(crosses to B and kneels)

*(looking frantically for sword which
is under B, B hands F sword, F stabs
himself, falls across B to "die")*
*(all the players come C to bow and
the "audience" onstage applauds)*

BOTTOM:
Will it please you see the
epilogue?

(stepping forward, addressing Th)

THESEUS:
No epilogue, I pray you; your play
needs no excuse. For when the players
are all dead, there need none to
be blamed. *[players exit]* Lovers to
bed: 'tis almost fairy time. *[they exit and
the fairies enter]*

(more applause)
(players gather props and leave UR)
(they all exit UL)

TITANIA:
Hand in hand, with fairy grace, we
will dance and bless this place.

*(fairies tiptoe on from DL and
DR, take hands, form a circle)*

OBERON:
   So shall all the couples three
   Ever true in loving be;
   Trip away; make no stay:
   Meet me all by break of day.
[they exit]

*(leads fairies back and forth in
a circle dance)*

(scatter off in all directions)

PUCK:
If we spirits have offended,
Think of this and all is mended:
That you have just slumbered here,
While these visions did appear.
Honest puck, they do me call,
So good night to you all.
[he exits]

Act Five · Scene 1 **original abridged**	Act Five · Scene 1 **stage directions**
PUCK: If we shadows have offended Think but this, and all is mended, That you have but slumbered here, While these visions did appear. Honest Puck, they do me call, So good night unto you all. *[he exits]*	*(alone C stage* *speaking directly to audience)* *(bows and exits UC)*

(We have selected our punctuation based on the First Folio, the Fisher Quarto, and Staunton's "The Plays of Shakespeare" (1858–1861). We have taken some minor liberties with Shakespeare's text to accommodate our abridged version and, for this, we apologize to purists, to scholars and, most of all, to Shakespeare!)

"To what end are all these words?"
(a discussion of the language in Shakespeare's plays)

Having read the play, let's take a little time to look at Shakespeare's language—very different from the way we speak today?

Language evolves over the course of time. Foreign influences, developments in technology, new slang and altered usages of words all affect the way we communicate. What is perfectly clear in 1995, might be almost incomprehensible by the year 2395.

At the time that Shakespeare wrote, English was evolving at a particularly furious pace.

In 1066, England had been conquered by Frenchmen (Normans) who made French the official language of England. The upper classes spoke French, the lower classes spoke English (which was at that time a kind of German called Saxon) while all church business was conducted in Latin.

Over the course of time, a melding of these language occurred. And along with this, came a new national identity and pride. The inhabitants of England no longer thought of themselves as Saxons or Frenchmen but as *Englishmen.*

By the time Henry V reestablished English as the official language of the land around 1400, English was evolving into a new and extremely exciting vehicle for communication.

New words and new ways of saying things became the mark of a clever person.

It was into this atmosphere that Shakespeare was born. By the time Shakespeare had come along, language was not merely a tool used to get through the day, but a song to be sung, a flag to be waved, capable of expressing anything and everything. It was a kind of national sport. The basic rules had been laid down and now the sky was the limit. Everyone was a *rapper,* a *wordsmith.* And Shakespeare was better at this game than anyone of his time and perhaps since. It is said that Shakespeare added over a thousand 'new' words to the language.

Getting 'easy' with Shakespeare is like learning to read or drive; once you get the hang of it, your world is changed.

Language is the 'guardian' at the entrance gate to the land of Shakespeare. To enter, one must tame the guardian. This simply means that you must take the time to become familiar with his ways.

And now for the good news, once you learn the guardian's way, he changes. He ceases to be an obstacle and instead becomes your guide and ally; your conveyance to Shakespeare's world and mind.

Let's examine a few of the techniques that will help you to tame the guardian and make your exploration of Shakespeare easier.

1) The first thing to do is to find out what all the words mean. In order to do this, you will want to go to your local library and gather any Shakespeare lexicons or glossaries, and as many different dictionaries and thesauri you can locate, along with all the versions of *A Midsummer Night's Dream* (with their various footnotes and explanations) and look up all the words you don't know. Note their various meanings and try to determine which best fits the context you found the word in.

2) We must remember that Shakespeare, as well as other poets, take poetic license—they will allow themselves to deviate from accepted form in order to achieve a desired effect. Poets will often rearrange words to acheive a more musical, poetical structure, or perhaps to get a rhyme to occur at the end of a line. Sometimes, by merely rearranging the subject, verb, adverbs, etc., into the order we are used to today, we can clarify the meaning of an otherwise complicated sentance.

An example of this can be seen with Philostrate's line in Act 5 scene 1:

A play there is, my lord, some ten words long
Which is as brief as I have known a play,
But by ten words it is too long.

We see that by merely inverting the first line to:

There is, my lord, a play some ten words long,
the meaning becomes perfectly clear to us.

3) Another thing Shakespeare does, is to take words and *stretch* their obvious meanings. He will use a word in a correct, but somewhat unusual manner so that he makes us see something in a whole new light and thereby broadens and enrichens our view of the world.

Look for example at Lysander's description of Helena after he has fallen in love with her under the influence of the love-juice:

LYSANDER:
Fair Helena! who more engilds the night
Than all yon fiery oes and eyes of light.

Here, Shakespeare has taken the words "oes" and "eyes" and used them in an entirely new way. An "o" is a little circle. An "eye" is what we see with. Yet Shakespeare has chosen these words to describe the light emitting from the stars in the night sky. He is making us see a skyful of little "oes" and "eyes" blinking and twinkling away at us. And Helen's beauty, according to Lysander, is shining more brightly than all of these stars put together.

Will we ever be able to look up into the night sky again without thinking of this image? This is the amazing impact that Shakespeare can have on us.

When we come across a situation like this, we must look at the context of the unusual usage and use our imaginations to stretch the meanings of the word as Shakespeare might have done. Once we start thinking like Shakespeare, we can open ourselves to the various shades of meaning contained in words.

4) Shakespeare's use of the apostrophe sometimes makes words seem strange to us, but when we realize that he is using it no differently than we do in modern English, the words become easy to understand.

An apostrphe merely tells us that there is something missing—for example, i the word "I'll"—the apostrophe replaces the "wi" —"I'll" is a contraction for "I will." So with Shakespeare, the word "o'er" means "over." Shakespeare often contracts words in this manner to alter the number of syllables in a line in order to fit his poetic structure.

5) Yet another thing to keep in mind when dealing with Shakespeare, is that most of the punctuation in the versions you will read was put there by an editor in subsequent centuries and was not Shakespeare's.

Quite frankly, Shakespeare was more concerned with meaning than with grammatically correct punctuation. He was writing for actors and his objective with punctuation was to clarify how an actor should interpret a line. In fact, it is thought that many of the actors in Shakespeare's company could not read and that the learning of a script was a verbal process.

Therefore, a good way to get more comfortable with Shakespeare might be to listen to professional actors on recordings of Shakespeare's plays and follow along in a script. Don't be afraid to imitate what you hear, it is an excellent way to learn.

6) We find though, that the very best way to become comfortable with Shakespeare and his language is to work with the material out loud. There is something marvelous that happens when we speak the words that helps to clarify their meanings.

Merely reading about baseball rarely improves your technique—so with Shakespeare, his material was meant to be performed, and therefore, the best way to connect to and understand the material is to speak it out loud, preferably with other people, but even alone works wonders.

You'll be amazed to discover Shakespeare's language becoming clearer and clearer as you work this way. Just remember; patience and practice!

Taming the guardian

This exercise is designed to put into practice the various techniques for understanding Shakespeare that we have just talked about.

Select one of the following speeches (which are from *A Midsummer Night's Dream* and have either been cut or not used in their entirety in our version of the play) and *translate* the speech into vernacular American.

This is the time to go to the library and locate all those reference books that we talked about earlier and look up all the words in the speech you've chosen.

You might want to do this working as a group or in pairs, sharing your ideas as you work. Or, you might work individually on the same speech and then compare results after.

Once you have found the various meanings of the words, and made lists of them, you can begin to select the ones that seem most appropriate for conveying the meaning of the speech.

Note that you may also need to rearrange the order of words to clarify the meaning.

Now put this all together and write a vernacular version of the speech. When doing this, try to imagine the words that the character who speaks the speech in the play, might use if he or she were speaking today.

Remember, there are no right or wrong ways to do this exercise. Be creative and daring. Shakespeare certainly would be if he were around today and had our version of the English language to work with!

Now that you have broken the code and the guardian is starting to seem friendlier, go back to the original version of your speech and read it aloud keeping strongly in mind the meanings of the words that you have now discovered.

Note how much clearer Shakespeare's language has become for you and for your listeners. This is the fact that every actor knows; *the clearer the understanding of the language, the more clearly it will be conveyed.*

Note too, how well Shakespeare says things—in such a way that pretty much sums it up. It is not only the words he chooses, but the order he has selected to put them in, that creates the incredibly rich imagery that he is so famous for. You could say it differently perhaps, but not better!

This is why, while it is possible to update the language, with vernacular versions, it is certainly never preferable to use them for any reason other than as a tool for getting back to the original.

He is the Master!—and now that you are learning how to tame the guardian, you will be able to enter into Shakespeare's world and begin to discover the breadth and depth of his insights into human nature.

[You will note that for this exercise, we have printed Shakespeare's text in *verse form*. This is the way you will find Shakespeare's works commonly printed. We have chosen not to use the verse form in our cut version for reasons of simplicity, but now that you have become more familiar with Shakespeare and his language, it might be a good idea to get used to it. When dealing with the verse form, do not stop at the end of the line unless there is punctuation telling you to. If there is not a period or a colon, continue reading on until the thought is complete. Also, don't be thrown by the fact that each line begins with a capitalized letter, this is merely part of the form.]

Egeus: (Act 1 scene 1, accusing Lysander
of stealing Hermia's heart)
 Thou hast by moonlight at her window sung,
 With feigning voice, verses of feigning love;
 And stol'n the impression of her fantasy
 With bracelets of thy hair, rings, gauds, conceits,
 Knacks, trifles, nosegays, sweetmeats; messengers
 Of strong prevailment in unhardened youth.

Theseus: (Act 1 scene 1, advising Hermia
of her filial responsibilities)
 Be advised, fair maid:
 To you, your father should be as a god;
 One that composed your beauties; yea, and one
 To whom you are but as a form in wax
 By him imprinted, and within his power
 To leave the figure, or disfigure it.

Theseus: (Act 1 scene 1, describing the
nun's life to Hermia)
 Thrice blessed they that master so their blood,
 To undergo such maiden pilgrimage:
 But earthlier happy is the rose distilled,
 Than that, which, withering on the virgin thorn,
 Grows, lives, and dies, in single blessedness.

Theseus: (Act 1 scene 1, exiting from the first scene)
   what cheer, my love?
 Demetrius, and Egeus, go along:
 I must employ you in some business
 Against our nuptial; and confer with you
 Of something nearly that concerns yourselves.

Helena: (Act 1 scene 1, Helena telling Hermia how
much she envies her)
 My ear should catch your voice, my eye your eye,

 My tongue should catch your tongue's sweet
  melody.
 Were the world mine, Demetrius being bated,
 The rest I'll give to be to you translated.

Hermia: (Act 1 scene 1, Hermia, telling how her love
for Lysander has altered her feelings for her home-
town)
 Before the time I did Lysander see,
 Seemed Athens as a paradise to me:
 O then, what graces in my love do dwell,
 That he hath turned a heaven unto a hell!

Lysander: (Act 1 scene 1, telling Helena when he and
Hermia plan to elope)
 Tomorrow night, when Phoebe doth behold
 Her silver visage in the wat'ry glass,
 Decking with liquid pearl the bladed grass,
 (A time that lovers' flights doth still conceal,)
 Through Athens' gates have we devised to steal.

Helena: (Act 1 scene 1, musing on Love)
 Love looks not with the eyes, but with the mind,
 And therefore is winged Cupid painted blind.
 Nor hath Love's mind of any judgment taste,
 Wings, and no eyes, figure unheedy haste;
 And therefore is Love said to be a child,
 Because in choice he is so oft beguiled.
 As waggish boys in game themselves forswear,
 So the boy Love is perjured everywhere.

Titania: (Act 2 scene 1, describing some of the prob-
lems the world is experiencing due to her and
Oberon's fighting)
 Therefore, the winds, piping to us in vain,
 As in revenge, have sucked up from the sea
 Contagious fogs; which, falling in the land,
 Hath every pelting river made so proud,
 That they have overborne their continents.

Titania: (Act 2 scene 1, talking about her friend
who has died)
 His mother was a vot'ress of my order:
 And, in the spiced Indian air, by night,
 Full often hath she gossiped by my side,
 And sat with me on Neptune's yellow sands,
 Marking th' embarked traders on the flood;
 When we have laughed to see the sails conceive,
 And grow big-bellied, with the wanton wind:
 Which she, with pretty and with swimming gait,
 Following, (her womb then rich with my young
  squire,)
 Would imitate; and sail upon the land,
 To fetch me trifles, and return again,
 As from a voyage, rich with merchandise.

Demetrius: (Act 2 scene 1, explaining to Helena why she should not pursue him any further in the forest)
>You do impeach your modesty too much,
>To leave the city, and commit yourself
>Into the hands of one that loves you not;
>To trust the opportunity of night,
>And the ill counsel of a desert place,
>With the rich worth of your virginity.

HELENA: (Act 2 scene 1, explaining to Demetrius why she feels safe with him in the forest)
>Your virtue is my privilege; for that
>It is not night, when I do see your face,
>Therefore I think I am not in the night:
>Nor doth this wood lack worlds of company,
>For you, in my respect, are all the world:
>Then how can it be said, I am alone,
>When all the world is here to look on me?

Lysander: (Act 2 scene 2, trying to convince Hermia that it is proper for them to sleep next to each other)
>O, take the sense, sweet, of my innocence;
>Love takes the meaning, in love's conference.
>I mean, that my heart unto yours is knit,
>So that but one heart we can make of it:
>Two bosoms interchained with an oath;
>So then, two bosoms, and a single troth.
>Then, by your side no bed-room me deny,
>For, lying so, Hernia, I do not lie.

Lysander: (Act 2 scene 2, explaining to Helena why he was not mature enough till now to love her)
>Things growing are not ripe, until their season:
>So I, being young, till now ripe not to reason.
>And touching now the point of human skill,
>Reason becomes the marshal to my will,
>And leads me to your eyes, where I o'erlook
>Love's stories, written in love's richest book.

Helena: (Act 2 scene 2, rejecting Lysander's overtures of love to her)
>Is't not enough, is't not enough, young man,
>That I did never, no, nor never can,
>Deserve a sweet look from Demetrius' eye,
>But you must flout my insufficiency?

Lysander: (Act 2 scene 2, explaining why he no longer feels he loves Hermia)
>For, as a surfeit of the sweetest things
>The deepest loathing to the stomach brings;
>Or, as the heresies that men do leave,
>Are hated most of those they did deceive;
>So thou, my surfeit, and my heresy,
>Of all be hated, but the most, of me!

Bottom: (Act 3 scene 1, talking to Mustardseed about the drawbacks to being a foodstuff)
>Good Master Mustardseed, I know your patience well. That same cowardly, giantlike ox-beef hath devoured many a gentleman of your house. I promise you, your kindred hath made my eyes water ere now. I desire you more acquaintance, good Master Mustardseed.

[Note that the above section is not written in verse; Shakespeare often switches between verse and prose in the course of a play.]

Hermia: (Act 3 scene 2, accusing Demetrius of having murdered Lysander in his sleep)
>Henceforth be never numbered among men!
>O, once tell true, tell true, even for my sake;
>Durst thou have looked upon him, being awake,
>And hast thou killed him sleeping? O, brave touch!
>Could not a worm, an adder, do so much?
>An adder did it; for with doubler tongue
>Than thine, thou serpent, never adder stung.

Lysander: (Act 3 scene 2, trying to convince Helena that his love for her is sincere)
>Why should you think that I should woo in scorn?
>Scorn and derision never come in tears.
>Look, when I vow, I weep; and vows so born,
>In their nativity all truth appears.
>How can these things in me seem scorn to you,
>Bearing the badge of faith to prove them true?

Helena: (Act 3 scene 2, accusing Lysander and Demetrius of making fun of her)
>You both are rivals, and love Hermia,
>And now both rivals, to mock Helena:
>A trim exploit, a manly enterprise,
>To conjure tears up in a poor maid's eyes
>With your derision! None of noble sort
>Would so offend a virgin; and extort
>A poor soul's patience, all to make you sport.

Hermia: (Act 3 scene 2, explaining how she managed to find Lysander in the dark)
>Dark night, that from the eye his function takes,
>The ear more quick of apprehension makes:
>Wherein it doth impair the seeing sense,
>It pays the hearing double recompense.
>Thou art not by mine eye, Lysander, found;
>Mine ear, I thank it, brought me to thy sound.

Helena: (Act 3 scene 2, accusing Hermia of encouraging Lysander to make fun of her)
>   And wherefore doth Lysander
>Deny your love, so rich within his soul,
>And tender me, forsooth, affection;

But by your setting on, by your consent?
What though I be not so in grace as you,
So hung upon with love, so fortunate;
But miserable most, to love unloved!
This you should pity, rather than despise.

Helena: (Act 3 scene 2, accusing all three of her
friends of mocking her)
Ay, do, persever, counterfeit sad looks,
Make mouths upon me when I turn my back,
Wink each at other, hold the sweet jest up:
This sport, well carried, shall be chronicled.

Puck: (Act 3 scene 2, explaining to Oberon why he
thinks they must conclude their business hastily)
My fairy lord, this must be done with haste;
For night's swift dragons cut the clouds full fast,
And yonder shines Aurora's harbinger;
At whose approach, ghosts, wand'ring here and
    there,
Troop home to churchyards.

Oberon: (Act 3 scene 2, explaining to Puck that they
are different from other spirits)
But we are spirits of another sort:
I with the morning's love have oft made sport;
And, like a forester, the groves may tread,
Even till the eastern gate, all fiery red,
Opening on Neptune with fair blessed beams,
Turns into yellow gold his salt-green streams.
But, notwithstanding, haste; make no delay:
We may effect this business yet ere day.

Oberon: (Act 4 scene 1, removing the spells from
Titania and Bottom)
                    I will undo
This hateful imperfection of her eyes.
And, gentle Puck, take this transformed scalp
From off the head of this Athenian swain;
That he awaking when the other do,
May all to Athens back again repair,
And think no more of this night's accidents,
But as the fierce vexation of a dream.

Bottom: (Act 4 scene 2, instructing his fellow 'actors'
on how to prepare for their upcoming performance)
In any case, let Thisbe have clean linen: and let not
him that plays the lion pare his nails, for they shall
hang out for the lion's claws. And, most dear actors,
eat no onions, nor garlic, for we are to utter sweet
breath: and I do not doubt but to hear them say, it is a
sweet comedy.
[note: the above is prose, not verse]

Theseus: (Act 5 scene 1, his explanation of why
'lovers' are slightly cuckoo)
The lunatic, the lover, and the poet,
Are of imagination all compact:
One sees more devils than vast hell can hold—
That is the madman: The lover, all as frantic,
Sees Helen's beauty in a brow of Egypt.
The poet's eye, in a fine frenzy rolling,
Doth glance from heaven to earth, from earth to
    heaven;
And, as imagination bodies forth
The forms of things unknown, the poet's pen
Turns them to shapes, and gives to airy nothing
A local habitation and a name.

Theseus: (Act 5 scene 1, sending everyone off to bed
after the play has been performed)
I fear we shall outsleep the coming morn,
As much as we this night have overwatched.
This palpable-gross play hath well beguiled
The heavy gait of night. Sweet friends, to bed.
A fortnight hold we this solemnity,
In nightly revels and new jollity.

Oberon: (Act 5 scene 1, instructing the fairies to bless
the marriage beds)
Now, until the break of day,
Through this house each fairy stray.
To the best bride-bed will we,
Which by us shall blessed be:
And the issue there create,
Ever shall be fortunate.

The rehearsal process
(who's who and what's what in putting a play together)

WHO'S WHO:

There is first of all the play, then the actors, then the director. The job of the director is to make sure the story gets told. This can entail many elements: working with actors to help them develop their characters, making sure each actor is headed in the right direction, maintaining order in the rehearsal so that work can move along smoothly, assigning people to do props, costumes etc.

The director is ultimately the benign dictator who makes sure everything comes together at the right time—that's why they get the big bucks!

The stage manager is the director's right hand—a combination of sergeant at arms and girl friday.

Among the stage manager's many jobs is: recording the blocking in a master script, prompting the actors when they forget their lines (that means a stage manager must always be following along in the script during rehearsals), making sure everyone is at rehearsal on time, coordinating the technical elements (props, costumes, etc.), calling break times and gathering everyone together after the break, helping the director maintain an orderly rehearsal, and once the show is in performance, the stage manager must make sure everyone and everything is in the proper place to insure the show will run smoothly, and most importantly, never becoming frazzled!

The stage manager can usually use an assistant or two. Give careful consideration when selecting someone for this position—a good stage manager is invaluable!

CASTING THE PLAY:

The first thing we need to do is to *cast* the play; that is figure out who will play which role. This can be done by having *auditions* for the parts. To do this, people read various scenes from the play and then the director, teacher or the other members of the class make determinations of who would be best suited to play a certain role.

Another way to cast is to have the teacher assign roles. Sometimes it is fun to have multiple casts (more than one actor for each part) that way actors can share their ideas in rehearsal and learn from each other.

With multiple casting, the play could then be presented more times in order to give everyone a chance to *read* or perform.

Something to keep in mind when casting, is that an obvious choice for a role may not always be the best one. Sometimes a male part might be better played by a female actor or visa versa. Or an actor whose physical characteristics are not exactly what's called for, might actually be able to bring something more interesting to a certain part. So remember to be flexible and open-minded in the casting process.

INVESTIGATING THE SCRIPT:

Once the casting is determined, it's time to get to work. Professional actors usually begin the rehearsal process by sitting around together and reading the play out loud a number of times.

The first time through, we just listen to the story. The next time through we start discussing the play.

The rules here are usually that anyone may stop and ask a question at any time. It could be a question of the meaning of a word, a discussion of why a character does something, or perhaps a question about where a scene is taking place.

In other words, everything and anything that may not be perfectly clear should be examined at this point.

This is done to make sure that everyone fully understands what is being said and what is going on in the course of the play.

This can take days or even a week in a professional company (and that's working eight hours a day!) So take your time on this step and be thorough.

The more time spent clarifying everything at this stage of the process, the more smoothly the rest of the rehearsal will go.

Once all the questions have been answered, go back and read the play again and note how much richer and clearer the language will be to you.

At this point the decision must be made whether you are going to do a *reading* of the play or a simple production. A reading is a modified performance in which there would be no sets or costumes and is usually done with only the simplest movement. Actors could just be seated in a semicircle, facing the listeners, with their scripts in hand and read the play.

DOING A READING:

If you have decided upon a reading, you still must determine how best to tell the story of the play to make it clear and interesting for the audience.

This is done by adding *shape* or *structure* to our work. We do this by going scene-by-scene through the play and (having determined what the scene is about in our previous work) figuring out how it fits into the overall arc of the play, how that scene moves the story forward and how each character contributes to that movement.

By examining the scenes in this way, we can then determine the *rhythms* that the scene requires for the acting of it: for example, some will need to be fast-paced, some slow, some a combination of both; some will need to be quiet, some raucous; in some, the characters will speak quickly–perhaps overlapping the previous speaker, and in others, the language will be languid or perhaps romantic.

All these various elements will add what we refer to as *shape* and *color* to the material.

We do this with each scene and slowly expand our work to include larger sections, till the entire shape of the play becomes clear. Experiment, explore and see what works best for your production.

The director makes the final decisions because he or she will have the best overview of the play, having been able to watch it all.

The most important element for a reading is a clear understanding of the language, the situation (or story) and the character relationships. These are after all, the most critical elements of Shakespeare.

This would be an excellent place for most classes to get to. But for those of you who wish to do a simple staging of the play, read on.

BLOCKING:

If you have decided to stage a production of the play, you still must do all the work of *shaping* discussed in the reading section, only you do this while *blocking* the play.

Blocking is the process of organizing the physical movement of the play. We usually block working one scene at a time and holding our scripts (that is before beginning to memorize our lines.)

The reason we do this, is because most actors find it much easier to memorize lines when the lines are connected to movements. (Note that the blocking we have offered with the text is merely one way to go, feel free to create movement that feels comfortable for you.)

WORKING SCENES AND MEMORIZING:

The next step would be to *work scenes* of the play–that is to rehearse them, adjusting the blocking as needed to make sure the actors feel comfortable with the movement and checking that the situations in the text are being properly clarified. It is during this step that we also begin memorizing the lines.

Memorization usually begins to happen on its own at this point, particularly if all the previous discussion work has been thoroughly accomplished. Shakespeare writes so well that his words seem to become the only

ones to say in the situations that he has devised. This is not the case with all playwrights!

There are times though (particularly with longer speeches) when it is necessary to go over and over a section out loud until it is ingrained in the brain and in the muscles of the mouth. (It's amazing how many times on stage, an actor has forgotten a line but his or her mouth still keeps going and knows what to say!) If an actor forgets a line during rehearsal, he or she says the word "line" and the stage manager (who is following along in the script) reads the line to the actor and work goes on.

This period of rehearsal is the longest and most exciting part of the process. It is when we go over and over each scene, that the language and the actions truly become part of us and we grow to understand a little more about the characters and their situations each time through. It is over this period that it is often said we are *becoming* the character.

In a professional situation, we are lucky if we have four weeks to spend on this part of the process. So again, spend as much time as you can.

Once individual scenes begin to *take shape*, we start putting together larger chunks of the play. Perhaps doing three or four scenes in a row and beginning to feel the *flow* of the play and finding the *throughline* of the characters.

Don't forget that this is an ongoing process and that different actors have creative inspirations at different points in the rehearsal period.

If someone comes up with a new and exciting idea after blocking has been completed, experiment with it and be willing to change, if it turns out to be better.

This is the *creative process* and these are the very instincts and ideas that will make your production unique and wonderful.

RUN-THROUGHS:

It is at this point that we put the whole play together and go through it from beginning to end. It is during the *run-throughs* that we finally get to understand what is needed from us as actors to take our character from his or her starting place to where they end up in the play.

TECHS AND DRESSES:

It is now that we add the final elements of props and costumes (sometimes, we are lucky enough to have gotten these earlier in our rehearsal process and have been able to incorporate them sooner.) But we definitely need everything at this point! These are referred to as the *technical* elements of the production.

Remember, though that the ultimate element of any Shakespearean production is the incredibly wonderful language through which Shakespeare conveys his ideas. Keep it simple and clear and it will enlighten and uplift...Good show!

Developing a character
(an exercise for creating a character history)

When working on a play, an actor will usually create a *history* or *background* for his or her character. This is the story of the character's life. It is made up by the actor in order to gather insights into the character's psyche and better understand how that character will respond to the various situations that he or she is confronted with in the course of a play.

We create this story by examining the *givens* in the text (that is, the various hints that the playwright has written into or given in the script), and making lists of all the information that we gather.

These include:

A) Everything that is said about the character by other characters in the play.

B) Everything the characters says about him or herself.

C) An examination of the physical characteristics and the physical limitations that the playwright might have specified in the text.

In addition to this information, we get more by asking a series of questions about the character:

1) What does the character want? This is a twofold question:

    a) What does the character want in the big picture of life—does he or she want to be a movie star? to be rich? to be loved?

    b) What does the character want in each scene. In other words, what is he or she desiring the other characters to do or say?

2) How does the character go about getting those things?—does the character aggressively go after things or is he or she passive? will she "sell her grandmother"? is he honest and plodding?

3) How does the character react in various situations—with anger? passively? with compassion? etc.

4) How does the character feel about him or herself?

5) What is his or her environment or social situation? Is this character from a family of fourteen and ignored by everyone? is he or she from a big city? a small town? a rich family? a well-educated family? etc.

6) How does the character's mind operate? Is he or she quick-witted or slow? plodding or inventive? etc.

7) What is the character's journey through the play? In other words, what is that character like when we first encounter them and when and how does the character evolve, grow or change during the course of the play? Or does that character remain unchanged?

We find the answers to these questions by scouring the text and by creating answers with our imaginations when they are not available. This is precisely why no two actors can ever play a character the same way. Each actor has personally *created* that character!

We now take the *givens* we have discovered in the text and combine these with the various answers we have come up with to our series of questions and create from this raw material our character's history.

During rehearsal, we constantly refer back to this history to help us figure out our characters actions and responses to the various situations in the play.

Remember, there are no right or wrong ways to do this. Just be honest in your search and when in doubt, always go back to the text.

Acting techniques and theatrical conventions

For those of you considering doing a performance of the play, here are some basic acting techniques and theatrical conventions to keep in mind.

PACING SHAKESPEARE'S PLAYS:

It is generally agreed that in Shakespeare's day, his plays were performed with alacrity. The language moved and the action moved.

With Shakespeare, perhaps more than with any other playwright, there is an acting technique that dictates that as soon as the last line of one scene is spoken, the first line of the next scene comes in hot on its tail.

Language is, after all the critical element of Shakespeare and we want all the action to come *on the language*—that is, with the words—unless otherwise specified.

This does not mean that the actor has to feel rushed or be afraid to take pauses, it's just that for the most part Shakespeare is best performed without indulgence. As Hamlet says to the players:

"Speak the speech I pray you, as I pronounced it to you, trippingly on the tongue."

Another important element for our purposes in performing, requires that after exiting from the stage, an actor proceed quietly and unobtrusively around upstage to the next place where he or she will make an entrance and then silently watch the action on stage until it is time to reenter.

MONOLOGUES:

If your character has a monologue, you have some choices in how to deliver it.

Depending on the situation, you could either talk directly to the audience and share your *inner thoughts* with them, or you could do the speech as though you were *thinking out loud* and the audience is overhearing you.

ASIDES:

An *aside* is a bit of dialogue that the audience hears, but supposedly, the other characters on stage do not hear.

Puck's lines, when he comes on and sees the *actors* rehearsing "Pyramus and Thisbe" is an example of an aside.

These are usually best executed by the actor who has the aside saying it directly to the audience and the other actors going on about their business as though they don't hear it.

ANGLING OUT:

This is a theatrical convention for making sure that the audience can see the actors onstage.

In real life when two people talk to each other, they probably stand face-to-face, but on stage it is necessary to stand on an angle facing slightly out to the audience in order to be seen.

When standing on the sides of the stage it is often necessary for the actor who is nearest the outside to place him or herself a little below and on an angle to the actor who is closer to the center in order to make sure the audience can see the action.

This is definitely something to experiment with.

COUNTERING:

Countering is adjusting your position on stage to accommodate or balance a movement made by another actor: such as when someone joins a scene already in progress or when an actor is required to cross from one side of you to the other.

We do this in order to keep adequate spacing between the actors on stage so that the audience can get a clear view of the action.

LIGHTING/DARKNESS:

In Shakespeare's day, most of the performances of his plays were done during the day in an open air theater. Therefore, night (darkness) was established by the language of the playwright and by various actor *conventions.*

Darkness can be *established* by the actor perhaps staring wide-eyed to show how hard it is to see at night, or feeling around with arms extended to indicate the difficulty of maneuvering in the dark.

Unsure, tentative movement, tripping or knocking into things also establishes the situation. This can be done either comically or straightforwardly depending upon the effect desired.

This does not mean that the actor has to concentrate on this during the entire scene. It is usually *established* when he or she first enters into the scene and then the actor returns to more normal actions and perhaps just reestablishes it from time to time.

INVISIBILITY:

This is not your average stage situation, but Dream requires us to deal with it. We accomplish this *magic* by establishing a theatrical convention for it.

In this case, we suggest that Puck and Oberon snap their fingers whenever they wish to become invisible.

The first time this happens is when Oberon says, "I am invisible." If he says the line and then snaps his fingers, he will have *established* the convention and after that, whenever they wish to be invisible, they need only snap their fingers and the audience will understand what is happening.

SOUND EFFECTS:

Again, getting back to Shakespeare's day, there were no tape recorders. Sound effects were done by the actors offstage, or sometimes onstage as the case may be.

We suggest for our purposes that we follow Shakespeare's lead and perform our sound effects in this manner.

Whichever actor can best "hoot like an owl," gets to be the owl sound etc.

AD LIBS:

When the term *ad lib* is noted in a script, it indicates to the actor that he or she must make up some words or dialogue to fill the moment.

Ad libs are usually called for to *cover* an entrance or exit that would otherwise be inappropriately silent such as when the workmen all exit after Act 1 scene 2.

In this situation it would be more real for them to be saying "adieu," "goodnight," "till tomorrow" etc. rather than leaving in silence.

Remember that whenever an ad lib is called for, it must be appropriate to the character and to the time in which that character lived!

SINGING AND DANCING:

The key point here is: keep it simple!

Any agreed upon tune for the fairies' lullaby will work. Or, you might want to *recite* the words, or have some actors hum while others speak.

The same rules of simplicity apply to dancing.

PLAY WITHIN A PLAY:

The *play within a play* is a device that Shakespeare uses from time to time.

In the case of *Dream*, it affords the *actors* a chance to *ham it up* and throw in whatever comic business seems appropriate. For example: when Pyramus dies, he has the word "die" five times. Not only can these lines be said with much coughing, spasming and writhing but, if Bottom *dies* after saying "die" four times, then props himself up onto his elbow and counts to four on his fingers, realizes he hasn't said all his lines and says his fifth "die" and *dies* again, this is (with practice) a guaranteed laugh! Trust me!

'BOINGS':

This is a theatrical convention that we have devised especially for this play.

This is an example of *theatrical license.* It is not in the script, but we think it might be a charming comic effect if Puck were to make this or a similar noise and do some sort of hand gesture to indicate the casting of a spell when he puts the lovers to sleep.

Note that it will be even funnier if the lovers react appropriately by immediately yawning and dropping off to dreamland.

"Here's a marvelous convenient place for our rehearsal..."
(a suggested set)

For our purposes, a simple set that serves for all locales is best.

We suggest a bare space with one low platform in the upper left quadrant of the stage. This platform could be the teacher's desk with a wooden crate as a step-up to it, or perhaps a 4X6 sheet of plywood resting upon six wooden crates, or whatever else you can come up with to suggest an area where actors may sit and where Titania may sleep etc.

Entrances and exits need only be delineated by a strip of tape along the floor. When the actor crosses that line, he or she has *entered* or *exited* the stage.

We also suggest using two short stools, or perhaps wooden crates to serve as seats in the DR and DL portions of the stage. They should be set in such a way as not to disrupt traffic patterns on entrances and exits, and to allow actors to easily get around them.

With this and all other *technical elements,* simplicity is the key factor, because in Shakespeare, language is foremost! See page 98 for a set diagram.

"Get your apparel together"
(suggestions for costumes and props)

For our purposes, props and costumes should be kept to an absolute minimum. This will not only make it easier to produce the play, but it will keep our focus firmly on the language where it needs to be.

COSTUMES:

We think the most effective costuming would be jeans and different colored t-shirts for the various groups of characters:

the upper class Athenians—shades of pinks, reds, and purples (Theseus and Hippolyta would probably wear the purple to denote their status)

the workmen—brown t-shirts
the fairyworld—greens and blues (Puck might defy convention and wear a multicolored t-shirt, he's a rebel!)

PROPS:

Scripts for Quince—his is the complete copy—so a number of pages fastened together would serve, the individual scripts that he hands out need only be one or two pages each.

Scroll for Quince—a single sheet of paper.

Love-juice flowers for Oberon and Puck—real or fake flowers may be used, Oberon needs one that he can remove a petal from to hand to Puck.

Bubbles for First Fairy—the sort that come in a bottle with a wand for blowing *soap* bubbles. We suggest this in order to give the First Fairy a way to create *magic.*

Map for Lysander—a piece of paper with a simple map drawn on it or perhaps a large folding road map would be fun to use.

Asses head for Bottom—a ski mask with cardboard, cut-out ears attached.

Plaster for "Wall"—a piece of plasterboard with a rope connected so that Snout can hang it around his neck, or perhaps a brick that Snout can hold up with one hand while he creates a "cranny" with the other by making a circle with his thumb and forefinger for Pyramus and Thisbe to speak through. O.K.?

Almanac for Quince—small book that Quince can have in his pocket. (Or Quince might have a bookbag that he carries around with all his various scrolls, scripts and almanacs inside it—this is up to the actor.)

Roses for Titania—two or three thornless, real or fake flowers wound into a crown to place on Bottom's ass-head.

Lantern for Moonshine—either a real lantern, a lantern shaped flashlight, or even a half-gallon milk container that has cut-outs on the sides and a flashlight stuck inside.

Lion's head for Snug—a mop-head for the lion's mane and a tennis ball with a slit in it, painted lion-nose-color for the nose!

Shawl—a piece of fabric large enough for Flute to wear over his shoulders that is marked with red stains on one side only. After Flute drops the shawl, Lion pretends to chew on it then leaves it with the red-stained part of it showing.

Sword for Pyramus—could be a toy sword or just a stick that Bottom wears in his belt.

Glossary

THEATRICAL CONVENTION:
an agreed upon action (that may or may not be used in everyday life) which we *establish* on stage to convey something unusual that the script may require—for example:
1. Oberon becoming invisible
2. darkness, when the lights are on

ESTABLISH:
To *establish* is to set up a theatrical convention such as when Oberon snaps his fingers the first time to indicate that he is invisible. He is here establishing the convention and after this time, we know that when he snaps his fingers, he cannot be seen.

THEATRICAL LICENSE:
liberties we take with the script to achieve certain results that we as actors, directors or editors are going for

COMIC BUSINESS:
known as *schtick, latzi* or *bits;* these are physical actions that actors do onstage (often exaggerated) that are contrived to get the audience to laugh

BLOCKING:
the organized physical movement of a play

REHEARSAL PROCESS:
the time between the casting of a play and the opening.

READING:
an organized, rehearsed presentation of a play in which the actors read from the script rather than memorizing the lines. (Could be done seated or with simple movements.)

SHAPE:
a clear definable beginning, middle and end to a scene or to the entire play. (Also referred to as *arc.*)

THROUGHLINE:
this usually refers to the series of actions a character performs throughout the course of a play in quest of his desires.

STAGE:
the area designated as the space upon which the action of the play takes place.

VERNACULAR:
Vernacular is defined by Webster's as "using a language or dialect *native* to a region or country rather than a literary, cultured, or foreign language." For our purposes then, vernacular would be our everyday American-English.

ENTER:
to walk into the area referred to as the stage

EXIT:
to leave the stage area

CROSS: (often abbreviated "X")
to move across the stage to the area indicated by whatever stage direction follows the term (xing then means—'crossing' in the stage directions)

STAGE TERMINOLOGY:

(note that the following stage terminology is indicated from the point of view of the actor, onstage, looking out to the audience)

SR:

the abbreviation for *stage right.* This means towards the right side of the stage as viewed by the actor when facing an audience.

SL:

the abbreviation for *stage left*—towards the left side of the stage from the actor's point of view.

US:

upstage means towards the rear of the stage.

DS:

downstage is towards the front of the stage.

C:

the *center* section of the stage.

We combine these terms to describe all the various sections of the stage. For example:

DRC: means *down-right-center* which refers to the lower part of the stage to the right of center stage.

DLC: *down-left-center* is the opposite of DRC.

UR: *upstage-right* is the upper part of the stage on the right side.

Use the chart on page 101 to determine other designations. Note that all areas are *approximate* designations only—this is not an exact science!

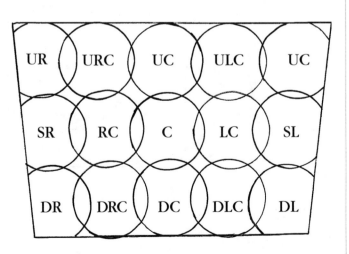

Additional Projects

1) Pick out a situation that is referred to in the play but not acted out and write an imaginary story to describe the incident, ie. describe the situation in whick Hermia and Demetrius first meet.

2) Write out a list of adjectives that describes the various aspects of your character.

3) Write out the story of what happens to your character during the entire course of the play.

In other words, don't limit your investigation to the time your character is onstage, but think about what is happening to your character when he or she is offstage.

4) Find out everything you can about Cupid.

5) Do research on the Amazons.

6) Find an Elizabethan tune that would be appropriate for the fairies' song (or write one!).

7) Research the legends of Theseus and Hippolyta.

8) Trace the history of Puck from its Celtic origins.

9) Write a love letter to the object of your heart's desire—in character!

You get the gist. Come up with a research project that interests you and pursue it. The more we know about a play and its elements, the better we understand and enjoy it!

Partial Bibliography

"The Story of English"
McCrum,. Cran and MacNeil
Viking Press 1986

"Shakespeare Lexicon and Quotation Dictionary"
Alexander Schmidt/revised Gregor Sarrazin
Dover Publications Inc. 1971

"A New Variorum Edition of Shakespeare—A Midsummer Night's Dream"
Ed. Horace Howard Furness
J.P. Lippincott Co. 1895

"Bankside Shakespeare—A Midsummer Night's Dream"
Ed. Appleton Morgon
The Shakespeare Society of New York 1890

"A Midsummer Night's Dream"
Ed. Sir Arthur Quiller-Couch and John Dover
    Wilson
Cambridge University Press 1968

"The New Folger Library Shakespeare A
    Midsummer Night's Dream"
Ed. Barbara A. Mowat and Paul Werstine
Washington Square Press 1993

"Asimov's Guide to Shakespeare"
Isaac Asimov
Avenel Books 1978

"The Plays of Shakespeare"
Ed. Howard Staunton
G. Routledge, 1858-1861

"The Arden Shakespeare—A Midsummer Night's
    Dream"
Edited by Harold F. Brooks
Methuen & Co. 1979

The Set

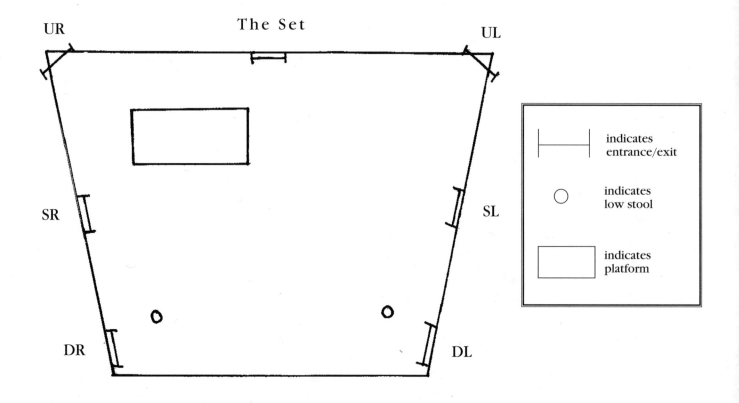